THE

QUIET

COLLAPSE

*Why Home Care Is Failing and
What Must Replace It*

by

BRIAN B. TURNER

For permissions, inquiries, or bulk orders, please contact:

hi@heybbt.com
www.heybbt.com

First Edition.
ISBN: *978-1-971050-00-3*

Printed in the United States of America

Disclaimer

This book is for educational and informational purposes only. It reflects the author's personal opinions, interpretations, and experiences in the home care industry. It is not intended to provide legal, financial, medical, or regulatory advice. Readers should consult qualified professionals before making decisions related to business operations, compliance, or patient care.

All references to companies, technologies, platforms, and industry trends are based on publicly available information and are included for commentary and analysis. They do not represent endorsements, partnerships, or verified statements from those organizations. Any similarities to specific individuals or agencies are coincidental.

The author and publisher assume no responsibility for actions taken based on the content of this book.

Table of Contents

INTRODUCTION.. 6

Chapter 1: The Workforce Has Left the Building........ 10

Chapter 2: Families Are Carrying the Weight Alone...18

Chapter 3: The Agency Model Cannot Survive............ 26

Chapter 4: The Franchise System: Too Big To Adapt..35

Chapter 5: The Caregiver Will Become the Center of the New Model...45

Chapter 6: The AI-Assisted Care Economy.................. 54

Chapter 7: The New Infrastructure of Care................. 62

Chapter 8: How AI Will Reshape the Core of Caregiving..71

Chapter 9: The CareFlow Framework: The Architecture of the New Model....................................82

Chapter 10: The New Role of the Caregiver: From Worker to Supported Professional................................ 92

Chapter 11: The New Experience for Families: Clarity Instead of Confusion.. 102

Chapter 12: The New Role of the Operator: From Administrative Burden to Strategic Leadership......... 112

Chapter 13: They Will Say This Will Not Work......... 122

Chapter 14: The AI-Assisted Care Model: How It Actually Works..135

Chapter 15: Why Intelligence, Not Infrastructure, Will Define the Next Era of Home Care..............................143

Chapter 16: What Caregivers Will Gain in the AI-Assisted Care Economy... 151

Chapter 17: The AI-Supported Caregiver.................. 160

Chapter 18: The AI-Supported Family...................... 169

Chapter 19: What the New Day Looks Like.............. 179

Chapter 20: Why Agencies Will Still Exist..................188

Chapter 21: What Families Will Pay For Now........... 197

Chapter 22: Where Agencies Will Lose If They Refuse to Change..207

Chapter 23: What the Next Decade of Home Care Will Look Like...218

Chapter 24: The System We Build Now....................... 229

EPILOGUE... 238

ABOUT THE AUTHOR.. 242

INTRODUCTION

The System Was Never Ready for What Came Next

For almost two decades, I have watched the home care industry argue, debate, and reorganize itself around the same problem. Everyone keeps asking how to save a model that was never designed for the world we are living in now.

Operators blame the workforce.
Franchisors blame the economy.
Families blame the agencies.
Agencies blame the reimbursement system.
And policymakers publish reports that say everything and nothing at the same time.

Meanwhile, the cracks keep widening.

Turnover climbs.
Workloads rise.
Margins shrink.
Families struggle.
Caregivers burn out.
And every year, more people need help at home than the system can possibly support.

I did not learn this from a conference or a white paper. I learned it from the inside.
From my own offices.
From my own caregivers.
From the families who called at 2 a.m.

From the auditors, the state surveys, the impossible scheduling weeks, and the never-ending race to hire faster than people quit.

The truth is simple.
The traditional home care model is collapsing.

Not because people do not care.
Not because operators are not trying.
Not because caregivers lack commitment.

It is collapsing because the system was built for a world that no longer exists.

We live in a different reality now.
Families are remote.
Care needs are rising.
Workforce supply is shrinking.
Documentation is heavier than ever.
Technology is moving faster than policy.
And the expectations of the next generation are not slowing down for anyone.

The model that carried us through the last twenty years will not carry us through the next ten.

This book is not a mourning.
It is a map.

A map of where home care is heading.
A map of how AI will reshape every layer of caregiving.
A map of how the workforce will shift from agency dependence to AI-supported independence.

A map of how families will demand visibility, transparency, and proof in real time.
And a map of why the biggest players in the industry are the least prepared for what is coming.

This is not theory.
This is trajectory.

The world is already moving toward the AI-assisted care economy.
Caregivers will not be replaced.
They will be empowered.
Families will not lose control.
They will gain clarity.
Operators will not disappear.
But the ones who remain will look nothing like the operators of the past.

This is the future of care.
Faster. Smarter. Safer. More human.
And built on the one thing the old model could never deliver at scale.

Support.

Quiet, real-time, always-on support.
For caregivers.
For families.
For anyone who steps into the responsibility of care.

If you have spent years in home care, you will recognize the fractures immediately.
If you are a policymaker, you will recognize the opportunity.

If you are a caregiver, this book will feel like relief.
And if you are an operator, it may feel like a warning.
Not because the future is dangerous.
But because it is different.

Radically different.

The collapse of the old model is not the end of
home care.
It is the beginning of a new one.

Let's talk about the world we are stepping into.
And why it is nothing to fear.

Chapter 1: The Workforce Has Left the Building

"A system will always break when the people holding it up can no longer carry it."

For years, the home care industry tried to avoid the truth that everyone inside the field already knew.

The workforce crisis did not suddenly appear.
It grew quietly, slowly, and steadily until the foundation of home care could no longer hold the weight being placed on it.

Caregivers did not leave because they stopped caring.
They left because the system stopped supporting them.

---

1. The Quiet Disappearance of the Workforce

The workforce crisis did not start with COVID.
It started long before.

For nearly two decades, caregivers have been asked to take on more responsibility with fewer resources.

Their workload increased while their wages stayed nearly stagnant.
Their documentation doubled while their support

stayed the same.
Their personal lives became more expensive while the job offered no real path for advancement.

The system did not collapse all at once.
It eroded.

Shift by shift.
Case by case.
Burnout by burnout.

Caregivers began walking away.
Not loudly.
Not angrily.
Quietly.

And the system barely noticed until the damage was irreversible.

---

2. The Work Has Become Heavier While the Pay Has Not

Every operator knows the truth.

The cost of living rose.
The expectations rose.
The acuity of clients rose.

But caregiver pay remained stuck between survival and struggle.

When you ask people to carry heavy work in light conditions, they can do it.

When you ask them to carry heavy work in crisis conditions, they collapse.

The job of caregiving now includes:

lifting
bathing
cooking
cleaning
dementia care
behavioral redirection
family dynamics
documentation
and emotional labor that no spreadsheet can measure

But the compensation never caught up with the responsibility.

Caregivers did not walk away from the work.
They walked away from the imbalance.

---

3. The System Became Too Complex for an Underpaid Workforce

Caregivers today must navigate:

apps
portals
forms
notes
timekeeping

tasks
safety protocols
family communication
and agency requirements

Each tool was added with good intentions.
But each addition increased the mental load.

Caregivers are human.
They can only juggle so much before something
drops.

The system gives them:

the responsibility of a nurse
the expectations of a social worker
the patience of a behavioral specialist
the documentation of an administrator
and the pay of an entry-level job

This model was doomed long before the labor
shortage showed up in the news.

---

4. Burnout Became the Default Setting

Caregivers left for the same reasons anyone would
leave.

They were tired.
They were overwhelmed.
They were unsupported.

They were blamed for systemic problems.
And they saw no future that looked different.

When an entire industry runs on exhaustion, people do not burn out.
They drain out.

One by one.
Month by month.
Year after year.

The shortage we see today is not a staffing issue.
It is a structural issue.

The system asks too much of people who receive too little.

---

5. The Workforce Shift Was Predictable

Operators saw it.
Families felt it.
Caregivers lived it.

It was predictable because the pressure points were obvious:

rising demand
rising acuity
rising living costs
falling wages compared to other industries
and a job that became more complex than the compensation could justify

When entry-level retail started paying more consistently than caregiving, the shift became inevitable.

This is not disrespect to caregivers.
This is economics.

People go where they can survive.

---

6. You Cannot Build a Future on a Workforce with No Future

The most overlooked truth is this:

Caregiving has no career ladder.

A caregiver can work for ten years:

no promotion
no advancement
no specialized pay
no clear pathway
no long-term incentives
no roadmap to grow
and no structure that honors the weight they carry

People do not leave because they do not care about the work.
They leave because the work has no future for them.

A system that depends entirely on human labor cannot survive when the humans holding it up have no reason to stay.

A model with no workforce cannot survive without intelligence supporting it.

---

7. The Workforce Crisis Is Not a Trend. It Is a Warning.

The workforce did not "dry up."
It migrated.

It moved to jobs with:

higher wages
less complexity
more stability
less emotional strain
better hours
and clearer paths forward

Caregiving did not lose its workforce.
The workforce lost its belief that caregiving would ever improve.

And until that changes, the crisis will continue.

---

8. Why This Matters for the Future of Care

Everything that follows in this book builds on this chapter.

You cannot design the future of home care without understanding why the present is collapsing.

A system cannot scale,
cannot modernize,
cannot innovate,
and cannot stabilize,

when the workforce is walking out the back door faster than agencies can recruit them through the front.

The workforce is not the problem.
It is the warning light.

A signal that the model itself is broken.
A signal that we must build something different.
A signal that the foundation must be rebuilt, not patched.

The future of care does not begin with technology. It begins with acknowledging why the people who carry the weight could no longer carry it.

The next chapter explores the other half of this crisis.

Because while caregivers walked away, families were quietly drowning in responsibilities they were never prepared to hold.

Chapter 2: Families Are Carrying the Weight Alone

"When a system weakens, the burden does not disappear. It shifts to the people least prepared to carry it."

Families were never meant to hold the level of responsibility they carry today.
Not the daily coordination.
Not the medical complexity.
Not the constant monitoring.
Not the emotional weight.

But as the workforce thinned and the system strained, families became the unofficial backbone of home care.

And they have been breaking under the pressure in silence.

---

1. Families Never Signed Up for This Much Responsibility

Most families step into caregiving gradually.

A small reminder here.
An appointment there.
A few household tasks.

A medication question.
A doctor's follow-up.

Then suddenly the responsibilities multiply.

A fall.
A hospitalization.
A memory change.
A new diagnosis.
A missed shift.
A weekend crisis.

Before they know it, they are managing the equivalent of a part-time job with no training, no guidance, and no margin for error.

Families did not become caregivers by choice.
They became caregivers by necessity.

---

2. The System Offloaded Its Weaknesses Onto Families

The home care model was built on the assumption that:

caregivers would always be available
agencies would always have backups
coverage would always be found
communication would always flow
and families would simply supplement the gaps

But when the workforce collapsed and agencies struggled to staff cases, the gaps widened into chasms.

Who filled them?

Not the system.
Not the agencies.
Families.

Families became:

the scheduler
the advocate
the backup plan
the crisis responder
the medication manager
the after-hours support
the emergency contact
and the person everyone calls when something goes wrong

The system didn't fail families loudly.
It drifted responsibility onto them quietly.

---

3. The Emotional Burden Became Its Own Form of Labor

Caregiving is not just physical work.
It is emotional work.

The fear of something going wrong.
The guilt of not doing enough.

The anxiety of coordinating everyone.
The pressure of being the decision maker.
The grief of watching decline happen in real time.

Families experience:

sleep disruption
constant worry
isolation
financial strain
role reversal
conflict with siblings
relationship pressure
and emotional fatigue that lingers long after the
day ends.

This is invisible labor.
Labor that no system measures.
Labor that no reimbursement model recognizes.
Labor that families carry alone.

---

4. Families Are Managing Care With Tools Never Designed for Care

Families try their best with what they have.

A notebook.
A shared calendar.
Group texts.
Screenshots of prescriptions.
Old discharge papers.

Voicemail updates.
Random instructions from different providers.

Nothing connects.
Nothing integrates.
Nothing communicates.
Nothing captures the full picture.

Families are forced to build a care system out of whatever tools they can find.

It is not sustainable.
It is not safe.
And it is not their fault.

---

5. When Agencies Struggle, Families Feel It First

When an agency is understaffed, families cover.
When documentation is missing, families improvise.
When a caregiver quits, families step in.
When a schedule falls apart, families rearrange their lives.

Families are now:

juggling work
raising children
managing households
caring for aging parents
handling medical updates
coordinating appointments
and filling the gaps left by the system

This is not support.
This is survival.

---

6. The Next Generation of Families Will Not Tolerate This

Millennials and Gen X are becoming the primary decision-makers for aging parents.

They are:

tech-driven
data-driven
time-poor
career-focused
and used to transparency in every other area of their lives

They book travel through an app.
They track health through a device.
They expect real-time updates in every service they use.

They will not accept:

unclear communication
paper-based care plans
inconsistent staffing
lack of visibility
or outdated systems

This generation will demand a different experience.

Not more people.
More clarity.
More support.
More intelligence behind the scenes.

---

7. Families Are Not Asking for Less Work. They Are Asking for Less Chaos.

Families understand care is complex.
They understand decline happens.
They understand that people get tired.
They understand caregiving is emotional.

They are not asking for perfection.
They are asking for predictability.

They want:

clear updates
accurate information
consistent staff
simple explanations
early warnings
and a system that does not require them to hold everything together.

They want care that feels manageable.
Not overwhelming.

---

8. Why This Matters for the Future of Home Care

Families were never trained for this role.
They never asked for it.
They never prepared for it.
But the system placed it on them anyway.

You cannot build the future of home care without
acknowledging the burden families have carried
alone.

If the next era of care does not:

lighten their load
organize their world
keep them informed
and make caregiving sustainable

then the collapse will continue no matter how
much technology enters the field.

Families are the second warning light.
The first was the workforce.
Both point to the same truth.

The model is breaking from both sides.

In the next chapter, we examine the structure that
sits between caregivers and families.
The layer that is supposed to hold everything
together, but no longer can.

Chapter 3: The Agency Model Cannot Survive

"A structure built to manage care cannot survive when the cost of managing it becomes heavier than the care itself."

Caregiving is simple.
Care management is not.

For years, the home care industry has depended on a model that places enormous administrative weight on the agency layer. It sits between caregivers and families and absorbs every task that does not fit neatly anywhere else. That weight has grown heavier each year while the agency's capacity to carry it has grown weaker.

The agency model is not failing because of bad leadership.
It is failing because it was never designed for the conditions it now faces.

---

1. Agencies Were Built for a Simpler Era

The original home care agency model was created in a world where:

families lived close by
care needs were lighter

documentation was minimal
technology was limited
workforce supply was steady
and regulatory expectations were low

Agencies could manage care with paper files, small teams, and predictable routines.

Nothing about today resembles that world.
Yet agencies are still expected to operate as if it does.

---

2. The Administrative Burden Has Outgrown the Agency Structure

Modern agencies are responsible for an overwhelming list of duties:

scheduling
coverage
onboarding
credentialing
documentation
compliance
electronic visit verification
training
payroll
billing
family communication
safety protocols
after-hours response
and constant crisis management.

In the traditional model, every layer of the system offloads its pressure onto the agency.

The administrative weight has scaled.
Agency capacity has not.

---

3. The Financial Math No Longer Works

Agencies operate on thin margins. Very thin.

Every cost increase hits the agency layer first, including:

ACA requirements
PTO mandates
rising wages
recruitment fees
background checks
EVV platforms
insurance premiums
overtime rules

Agencies absorb these costs because the system gives them no alternative.

Here is the truth, owners rarely say out loud:
You cannot pay caregivers the wages they deserve and keep the agency profitable without breaking the traditional financial model.

Margins shrink.
Turnover rises.

Coverage gaps widen.
Operators burn out.
Families feel the instability.
Caregivers feel the strain.

This is not a leadership issue.
It is an economic one.

---

4. Agencies Became the Buffer for a System That Never Evolved

Technology was supposed to take the weight off the agency.

Instead, agencies took the weight.

Technology was supposed to automate tasks.

Instead, agencies manually handled what the system did not innovate fast enough to solve.

Agencies became the buffer between:

caregiver expectations
family demands
payer requirements
regulatory changes
and outdated systems

They became the shock absorbers for problems that should have been solved by better tools.

Shock absorbers are not designed to last forever.

5. Documentation Now Takes More Work Than the Care Itself

The most overlooked shift in home care is the documentation explosion.

Agencies spend more time:

fixing EVV discrepancies
editing notes
tracking tasks
closing documentation gaps
checking compliance
auditing visits
and correcting errors

than they do support caregivers or families.

When the administrative engine requires more fuel than the care engine, collapse becomes inevitable.

6. Scaling the Agency Model Made It Weaker, Not Stronger

In most industries, scaling creates efficiency.

In-home care, scaling creates fragility.

When agencies grow, they add:

more coordinators
more recruiters
more supervisors
more platforms
more after-hours staff
more administrators

Each layer adds cost and complexity.

Growth does not create stability in the traditional model.
Growth creates vulnerability.

The bigger the agency, the more pressure it carries.
The more pressure it carries, the higher the risk of collapse.

---

7. The Agency Layer Has Become the Single Point of Failure

If one caregiver calls out, a family adjusts.
If one family struggles, caregivers adapt.

But if the agency collapses, everything collapses.

Scheduling
Documentation
Quality
Compliance
Communication
Case stability
All of it depends on the agency layer.

The system is built around a hub that is overloaded. Overloaded hubs fail first.

---

8. The Industry Knows the Model Is Breaking, but No One Wants to Say It

Everyone in home care feels the pressure.

Operators feel it.
Families feel it.
Caregivers feel it.
Franchisors feel it.
Policymakers feel it.

But the agency model keeps getting sold as stable because:

families want reassurance
referral sources expect confidence
franchisors need to sell territories
investors need predictability
and agencies need to appear strong to stay alive

Silence is not denial.
Silence is survival.
Silence does not make the model sustainable.

---

9. This Is Not About Blame. It Is About Structure.

The agency model is not collapsing because owners are failing.
It is collapsing because the model depends on:

manual processes
unpredictable labor
heavy documentation
tight margins
high burnout
and an aging population with rising needs.

It is a structure built for a world that no longer exists.

No amount of effort can compensate for a foundation that is fundamentally outdated.

---

10. The Truth at the Center of the Collapse

The core job of an agency is to:

support caregivers
inform families
fill schedules
maintain compliance
and stabilize cases.

The traditional model can no longer deliver these outcomes at scale.
The collapse is not emotional or dramatic.
It is structural, economic, demographic, and unavoidable.

11. Why This Matters for What Comes Next

Chapters 1 and 2 showed the weight caregivers and families now carry.
Chapter 3 reveals why the agency layer cannot continue holding everything in the middle.

You cannot build the future of home care on a structure that no longer fits the world around it.

The next chapter shifts the lens to the part of the system that should have led the evolution, but instead became its own barrier to change.

Chapter 4: The Franchise System: Too Big To Adapt

"Scale without innovation is not strength. It is delay."

Home care franchising was built for a different era. It thrived when the industry was growing slowly, competition was limited, and the workforce was stable. The franchise model offered structure, branding, and a repeatable playbook that helped new operators enter the field.

That era is over.

The world changed faster than the franchise systems did, and franchisors became too large, too slow, and too invested in their old architecture to evolve at the speed the industry now requires.

This chapter is not an attack.
It is an observation shaped by lived experience inside the system and by conversations with operators who understand the pressure but rarely speak it out loud.

---

1. A Model Built to Grow, Not to Evolve

Franchises were designed for expansion.

Grow territories.
Sell units.
Increase brand footprint.
Attract new owners.
Replicate the playbook.

The engine runs on growth.
What it does not run on is innovation.

Innovation disrupts the existing system.
Innovation requires new tools, new training, and new workflows.
Innovation threatens the revenue model that franchisors depend on.

Franchises became experts at replication.
Replication is not evolution.

The lack of evolution creates fragility.

---

2. The Franchise Playbook Is Outdated

Most franchisors still teach a playbook created more than a decade ago.

Call referral sources.
Visit facilities.
Network with discharge planners.
Host community events.
Hire recruiters.
Fill schedules.
Repeat.

This worked when:

caregiver supply was steady
family expectations were simple
documentation was light
and competitors followed the same rules.

It does not work in a world where:

caregiver supply is shrinking
families want transparency
documentation is complex
and technology moves faster than policy.

The playbook has not kept up with the modern landscape.

---

3. A Structure Dependent on the Agency Layer

Franchisors built their model on the assumption that the agency layer would remain strong enough to carry the weight of the system.

They assumed agencies could:

hire consistently
retain caregivers
absorb new costs
handle growing documentation
respond to after-hours calls
maintain compliance
and execute the full playbook.

But the agency layer is buckling under its own load.

The expectations never changed.
The conditions did.

A system cannot stay strong if its foundation is weakening.

---

4. Innovation Threatens the Franchise Revenue Model

Franchise systems depend on three financial pillars:

royalties
brand funds
and territory sales

AI-driven, decentralized, low-overhead care models threaten all three.

They reduce the need for:

physical offices
large admin teams
manual scheduling
territory boundaries
brand-centric operations

Innovation requires franchisors to redesign:

the fee structure
the support structure

the operational model
and the value proposition

Most franchisors are not built for that level of
transformation.

They are built to protect what already exists.

---

5. Private Equity (PE) Inflated the System Instead of Strengthening It

Private equity rushed into home care because the
demographics looked irresistible.

An aging population.
Recurring revenue.
Fragmented markets.
Consolidation opportunities.

PE firms began buying large blocks of franchises: 5,
10, even 20 at a time.

On paper, it looked strategic.
In reality, it created a structural bubble.

Here is why.

PE did not solve the workforce shortage.
They simply multiplied the number of territories
competing for the same limited supply.

PE added administrative complexity.
Ten franchises do not equal ten solutions.

They equal ten problems multiplied across one labor pool.

PE treated home care like retail.
But home care is not retail.
It is labor-driven, high-touch, and unpredictable.

PE relied on size as a safety net.
In home care, size increases fragility, not stability.

This bubble will not burst dramatically.
It will burst quietly as revenue stabilizes and labor pressure exposes the cracks.

This correction is structural, not personal.
You cannot scale a model that cannot scale.

---

6. Territories Matter Less Every Year

Franchises depend on territory maps.

The assumption is that families will choose services based on geography.
That assumption is fading.

Families want:

speed
clarity
trust
communication
and updates in real-time

They do not care which office they fall under.

Technology is erasing geographic restrictions.

AI will allow caregivers to operate across broader service areas with clear oversight and real-time visibility.

Territory maps designed in 2005 cannot compete with a digital care ecosystem that moves without borders.

The franchise system is tied to geography.
The future of care is not.

---

7. Franchises Are Too Large to Pivot and Too Slow to Transform

Innovation requires:

speed
risk
experimentation
technology
and structural change.

Franchise systems require:

consistency
predictability
manuals
compliance
and risk avoidance

These two forces rarely coexist at scale.

Every industry moving into a technology era faces this divide.

Blockbuster did not collapse because people stopped watching movies.
It collapsed because it was too large, too slow, and too invested in its old model to adapt to a new one.

The home care franchise system is living the same tension today.

The future requires agility, intelligence, and real-time decision-making.
Franchises require stability, uniformity, and manual processes.

The model itself cannot pivot at the speed the market now demands.

---

8. The Messaging Is Stable. The System Is Not.

Franchisors promote:

growth potential
brand leadership
territory opportunity
and national presence.

But behind the messaging:

turnover is rising
labor supply is shrinking
documentation is heavier
regulation is increasing
technology is accelerating
and operators are burning out.

A system can only absorb this much pressure for so long.

The break is not sudden.
It is gradual and predictable.

---

9. Why This Matters for What Comes Next

The franchise system shaped the last twenty years of home care.
It offered structure, stability, and a way for new owners to enter the industry.

But it is too large, too slow, and too committed to its past design to lead the next phase of caregiving.

The next decade will belong to models that are:

lighter
faster
smarter
more transparent
more flexible
and supported by real-time intelligence

The next chapter begins the shift toward what will replace the franchise model and why the center of the entire industry will move back to where it should have been all along.

Chapter 5: The Caregiver Will Become the Center of the New Model

"Every industry eventually returns to the person who holds the real value. In home care, that person has always been the caregiver."

The future of home care will not be built around offices, administrators, referral sources, territory maps, or franchise handbooks.

It will be built around the caregiver.

Not as an afterthought.
Not as a cost center.
Not as a replaceable part of the system.
But as the center of the entire care economy.

Caregiving has always relied on one truth.
Families do not fall in love with agencies.
They fall in love with the caregiver who shows up for them.

This chapter explains why the next decade will belong to the caregiver and why every system that refuses to recognize that shift will struggle to survive.

---

1. The Caregiver Is the Real Product

The home care industry often behaves as if the agency is the product. The brand, the office, the promises, and the marketing are treated as the value.

But families do not stay because of a logo.
They stay because of the person walking through the door.

Caregivers build trust.
Caregivers build consistency.
Caregivers build loyalty.
Caregivers build outcomes.

The future of care must reflect this truth more clearly and more directly.

---

2. The System Treated Caregivers as Labor Instead of Value

For decades, caregivers have been:

underpaid
undervalued
overworked
overscheduled
and viewed as interchangeable

They were treated as a cost to be controlled instead of a foundation to be strengthened.

This is why turnover exploded.
This is why burnout became normal.
This is why agencies struggled to stabilize cases.
This is why the entire system is cracking.

You cannot build a stable industry on a workforce
the model itself destabilizes.

The world is now shifting toward a design that
finally recognizes the value caregivers bring.

---

3. The Myth of the Caregiver-First Agency

Many agencies say they are caregiver-first.
Most are not.

Not because they do not care.
Not because they lack integrity.
But because the traditional model makes
caregiver-first impossible.

You cannot be caregiver-first when your structure
forces you to be:

paperwork-first
compliance-first
crisis-first
and margin-first

Agencies often want to put caregivers first, but the
system they operate in pulls them in the opposite
direction.

Schedules must be filled.
Documentation must be corrected.
Audits must be passed.
Coverage must be maintained.
Costs must be controlled.

The structure makes it almost impossible to elevate caregivers in the way families assume and caregivers deserve.

The next decade will correct this imbalance by removing the layers that pull attention away from the caregiver and returning the focus to the person who delivers the care, not the system that processes it.

---

4. The Next Generation of Families Will Choose the Caregiver, Not the Agency

Families of the next decade are:

more digital
more informed
more direct
more selective
and less patient with outdated processes

They will not tolerate:

long intake calls
manual scheduling
unclear updates

generic assignment
poor communication

They want transparency, simplicity, and accountability.

They want to see the caregiver.
Understand the caregiver.
Trust the caregiver.
Stay informed about the caregiver's work.

Caregiver-first is not a slogan.
It is where the demand is shifting.

---

5. Caregivers Want More Than a Job

The next generation of caregivers wants:

autonomy
flexibility
higher pay
clear expectations
stable schedules
and meaningful support

They want dignity in their work.
They want clarity in their role.
They want tools that help, not systems that overwhelm.

The traditional model was never built to give caregivers what they deserve.
It was built to manage them, not empower them.

The future belongs to systems that recognize caregivers as skilled professionals who deserve support, technology, and respect.

---

6. Technology Will Give Caregivers What the System Never Could

Caregivers do not need more meetings or more layers of supervision. They need support that is immediate, simple, and reliable.

Technology can provide:

real-time guidance
real-time answers
real-time visibility
real-time connection
real-time documentation
real-time alerts
and real-time updates for families

AI can:

translate care plans
prevent errors
flag safety risks
monitor tasks
document automatically

verify visits
and reduce stress

For the first time, caregivers will have tools that do
not just monitor their work but empower it.

---

7. The Rise of Caregiver Micro-Businesses

One of the most significant shifts of the next decade
will be the rise of caregiver micro-businesses.

Caregivers will become:

independent providers
professionals with AI-supported oversight
trusted partners to families
and operators of their own schedules

This shift does not reduce accountability.
It increases it.

Technology will handle:

documentation
compliance
training
verification
communication
and quality checks.

Caregivers will finally have the structure and tools
that agencies could never provide at scale.

Families will choose caregivers directly.
Caregivers will choose the homes they want to
serve.
AI will handle the complexity.

The power will move to the center.

---

8. Agencies Will Evolve or Become Optional

Agencies will not disappear.
They will evolve.

The agencies that survive will:

operate with lower overhead
offer real-time technology
automate documentation
lighten the administrative load
and support caregivers rather than control them

The heavy, office-first, coordinator-driven model will
not survive.
The AI-supported, caregiver-centered model will.

---

9. Why This Matters for the Future of Care

When the caregiver becomes the center:

care improves
family satisfaction rises
retention stabilizes

burnout decreases
documentation gets easier
and outcomes become measurable.

This is not the destruction of home care.
It is the return to what home care was always
supposed to be.

Human first.
Supported by intelligence.
Driven by the caregiver.
Strengthened by technology.

Caregivers have always been the heart of home
care.
The future will finally treat them that way.

Chapter 6: The AI-Assisted Care Economy

"Care will always be human. The infrastructure around it no longer needs to be."

The home care industry does not need more offices, more coordinators, or more paperwork. It needs something that the traditional system has never been able to offer.

It needs intelligence.

Not intelligence in the sense of replacing people, but intelligence in the sense of supporting them. The same way navigation supports drivers, translation apps support travelers, and automation supports modern industries that once ran entirely on manual labor.

Care is the last major sector still trying to operate without the level of intelligence that every other sector now depends on.

The next decade will change that.

---

1. The System Collapsed Because It Lacked Support

Caregivers did not collapse.
Families did not collapse.
Operators did not collapse.

The system collapsed.

And it collapsed because the structure around care never evolved to match the complexity of modern needs.

Home care remained:

manual
paper-heavy
over-layered
labor-intensive
and dependent on the office staff

while everything around it accelerated.

The collapse was never about effort.
It was about infrastructure.

You cannot build a twenty-first-century care system on twentieth-century tools.

---

2. AI Will Not Replace Caregivers. It Will Carry the Weight

AI will not hold a client's hand.
AI will not make breakfast.
AI will not comfort a family at midnight.

AI will not keep someone company in the final moments of their life.

Caregivers will always be the heart of the system.

What AI will do is carry the weight that breaks caregivers today:

documentation
compliance
scheduling
med reminders
care-plan breakdowns
task tracking
safety alerts
reporting
visit verification
and communication

Caregivers do not need to be replaced.
They need to be supported.

AI will finally provide that support.

---

3. AI Will Bring Certainty to a System Built on Uncertainty

Home care today is unpredictable.

Shift changes, last-minute cancellations, medication confusion, incomplete notes, unclear expectations, and disconnected communication create constant instability.

AI can stabilize what has always been unstable:

predict missed visits
flag safety risks
support chronic conditions
identify behavioral changes
summarize documentation
guide caregivers through tasks
notify families automatically
and prepare operators for issues before they
happen.

The industry has never had a system that sees
problems before people feel them.

That is what AI brings.

---

4. Families Will Have Visibility They Never Had Before

Families today operate in the dark.

They hope visits happen.
They hope tasks get completed.
They hope communication is clear.
They hope their loved one is safe.

AI will make home care transparent.

Families will see:

who arrived
what was done

what changed
what needs attention
and what the caregiver recommends.

Not as a sales feature.
As the new standard.

Families do not want more reports.
They want clarity.

AI gives them what agencies never could:
information without stress.

---

5. The System Will Shift From Reactive to Proactive

The traditional model reacts.
AI models anticipate.

The traditional model waits for problems.
AI sees the early signs.

The traditional model depends on people noticing patterns.
AI identifies patterns automatically.

The traditional model responds to the last crisis.
AI prevents the next one.

This shift alone will redefine caregiving.

---

6. AI Will Remove the Barriers That Prevent Scale

Home care could never scale because the administrative requirements grew faster than the care volume.

AI will remove the barriers that kept the industry small:

manual onboarding
manual scheduling
manual oversight
manual documentation
manual communication

AI-supported systems will allow:

leaner agencies
caregiver micro-businesses
family-directed care
and regional models without office-heavy overhead

For the first time, home care will be able to scale without collapsing.

---

7. AI Will Make Care More Human, Not Less

People fear that AI will make care colder or more clinical.
The opposite will happen.

AI will:

reduce confusion
reduce burnout
reduce stress
reduce paperwork
reduce manual errors
reduce communication delays.

Caregivers will spend more time caring and less time documenting.
Families will spend more time present and less time worried.
Operators will spend more time supporting and less time surviving.

Intelligence does not remove humanity from care.
It frees humanity to do what only humanity can do.

---

8. Why This Matters for Every Stakeholder in the System

AI-supported care is not a luxury.
It is the only structure that matches the reality we are living in.

Caregivers need support.
Families need transparency.
Operators need sustainability.
Policymakers need efficiency.
Payers need accountability.
Franchisors need evolution.
And communities need a model that can hold the weight of an aging nation.

The AI-assisted care economy is not a trend.
It is the next phase of care.

A phase where the work becomes lighter, the outcomes become clearer, and the system becomes something it has never been.

Predictable.

---

9. What Comes Next in This Book

In the chapters ahead, we will break down exactly how this new economy will function:

how caregivers will operate
how families will engage
how agencies will evolve
how oversight will work
how the CareFlow Framework transforms the system
and how every layer of care becomes stronger when intelligence carries the weight

This is where the book shifts from analysis to architecture.

The collapse has already happened.
This is the blueprint for what replaces it.

Chapter 7: The New Infrastructure of Care

"The future of care will not be built on offices and coordinators. It will be built on intelligence and flow."

The traditional home care model was built on physical infrastructure:

offices
administrators
coordinators
supervisors
manual processes
territory boundaries

The next phase of care will be built on digital infrastructure:

real-time guidance
automated documentation
predictive alerts
transparent communication
streamlined workflows
AI-supported scheduling
and caregiver-centered tools

The new infrastructure will not eliminate the human element.
It will strengthen it.

This chapter explains the blueprint that will support the next decade of caregiving and why it requires a complete shift in how the industry thinks about operations.

---

1. Offices Will Not Be the Center of Operations Anymore

The traditional model treats the office as the heart of the agency:

calls
scheduling
intake
paperwork
compliance
crisis management
coordination
and every administrative task.

But offices cannot scale because:

they rely on people
they are expensive
they create bottlenecks
and they slow down communication

The future will shift the center of gravity away from the office and toward the caregiver, supported by systems that move faster than office staff can.

Care will no longer revolve around a building.
It will revolve around real-time information.

---

2. Real-Time Intelligence Will Replace Manual Oversight

Agencies today rely on human oversight to:

catch problems
fix documentation
manage errors
call caregivers
respond to families
and hold everything together

This type of oversight collapses under scale.

AI-supported intelligence will:

review notes
flag mistakes
guide tasks
standardize expectations
predict issues
and notify the right people before escalation

Oversight will shift from manual to digital, and office teams will focus on the human work that cannot be automated.

---

3. Documentation Will Finally Become Automatic

Documentation is the hidden weight crushing caregivers and agencies.

AI will remove this weight by:

capturing tasks automatically
translating actions into care notes
summarizing visits
detecting changes
filling in required fields
and generating compliance-ready logs

This will free caregivers from paperwork and allow operators to focus on quality rather than correction.

The system will no longer depend on people spending hours documenting what they did.
The system will document itself.

---

4. Scheduling Will Become Dynamic Instead of Manual

Traditional scheduling is reactive:

calls
text threads
voicemail tag
coordinator burnout
and constant shifting.

The new infrastructure will use real-time availability and intelligent matching to:

pair caregivers with the right clients
anticipate coverage gaps
fill cancellations automatically
and reduce scheduling failures.

Scheduling will not be a crisis-driven job.
It will be a dynamic system.

This will stabilize coverage and reduce stress on
both caregivers and coordinators.

---

5. Families Will Interact With Care the Same Way They Interact With Modern Technology

Families today track everything:

packages
GPS locations
medical appointments
home security
device usage

But they cannot track care.

The new infrastructure will give families:

live updates
completed tasks
caregiver notes
safety alerts
behavioral changes
missed tasks
future recommendations.

Not as a luxury feature.
As the standard.

This visibility will eliminate the uncertainty that drives family frustration and operator burnout.

---

6. Training Will Become Embedded Into the Work Itself

Most caregiver training today happens:

in a classroom
in a long module
or in a single orientation session

It does not match how caregivers actually learn.

AI will embed training into the care moment:

meal preparation reminders
safe transfer instructions
hygiene guidance
medication rules
fall prevention cues
behavioral tips
and dementia care support.

Training will no longer be something caregivers complete.
It will be something they receive continuously.

This elevates care without overwhelming the caregiver.

7. Quality Will Become Visible and Measurable

Today, quality is based on:

intuition
client feedback
sporadic supervision
and isolated documentation

AI-supported systems will measure quality through:

task completion
consistency
patterns of behavior
professional communication
adherence to care plans
changes in client condition

Quality will become measurable, visible, and predictable.

This will redefine accountability without adding stress.

8. The Cost Structure of Care Will Change Completely

The traditional model carries heavy overhead:

offices
admin staff

schedulers
supervisors
manual processes
and layers of oversight.

The new model carries lightweight overhead:

AI-assisted workflows
streamlined staffing
automated documentation
smaller teams
and higher efficiency.

Costs will shift from labor-heavy administration to intelligence-heavy infrastructure.

This is the only way home care becomes scalable and sustainable.

---

9. This Is the Foundation the CareFlow Framework Will Build On

Everything described here is the groundwork for the CareFlow Framework, the operating model that will replace the traditional agency structure.

In the next chapters, we will break down:

how caregivers will operate
how families will engage
how safety will be guaranteed
how oversight will work
how agencies can evolve

and how the next decade of care will be built on intelligence rather than exhaustion

Care has always been human.
The infrastructure around it is what must evolve.

Chapter 8: How AI Will Reshape the Core of Caregiving

"Caregiving is human work. Everything that prevents caregivers from doing that work is the problem."

For years, the industry has tried to fix home care by adding more:

paperwork
processes
audits
platforms
and compliance layers

None of it worked because it did not solve the real issue.

The problem in home care has never been the people.
It has always been the load.

Caregivers are not struggling because they lack compassion.
Agencies are not struggling because they lack effort.
Families are not frustrated because they lack patience.

They are struggling because the system asks humans to carry out work that should no longer be done by humans.

Documentation.
Coordination.
Tracking.
Verification.
Communication.
Scheduling.
Monitoring.
Error correction.
Redundant reporting.

This is where AI enters the story.
Not as a replacement.
As relief.

I have watched caregivers, families, and operators fight against this weight in real time. It is not a lack of willingness. It is a lack of support. And support is where intelligence can finally do what the old model never could.

AI will reshape caregiving by removing the weight that has been crushing the industry for decades.

---

1. AI Will Not Replace Caregivers. It Will Replace the Tasks That Exhaust Them.

Caregiving is human.
Tasks are not.

AI will eliminate:

manual notes
paper care plans
checklists
time-consuming documentation
phone tag
coordination chaos
and constant verification

This will give caregivers their time, energy, and attention back.

Instead of fighting the system, they can focus on the client.

I have seen great caregivers walk away, not because of the work but because of the weight around the work. AI removes that weight.

AI will not take jobs.
AI will take burdens.

---

2. Real-Time Guidance Will Become the Standard

Today, caregivers navigate complex situations with:

unclear instructions
outdated plans
limited support
and guesswork based on experience

With AI-assisted support, caregivers will receive:

meal prep guidance
safe transfer reminders
dementia behavior tips
medication rules
fall prevention cues
nutrition prompts
mobility instructions

Not in a classroom.
In the moment.

Training will move from theoretical to practical.

Caregivers will no longer feel alone in difficult situations because guidance will be available instantly instead of waiting for a supervisor to call back.

This will elevate both confidence and consistency, two things the current model has never been able to deliver at the same time.

---

3. AI Will Identify Problems Before They Become Crises

The entire home care system today is reactive. Something goes wrong, and everyone hurries to respond.

Care is delayed.
Families panic.

Agencies scramble.
Caregivers feel blamed.

AI will shift the industry from reaction to prevention.

AI will detect:

changes in mobility
sleep pattern variations
unusual behaviors
missed meals
environmental risks
patterns of decline
task inconsistencies
communication drops.

This will allow issues to be addressed before they
escalate.

For the first time, care will move toward early
intervention, not damage control.

---

4. Communication Will Become Transparent
Instead of Fragmented

Families want clarity.
Agencies want stability.
Caregivers want direction.

But communication today relies on:

voicemail
text chains

email threads
and rushed updates

AI-supported communication will:

summarize visits
generate daily reports
flag critical changes
notify families
update care plans
and send alerts when tasks are incomplete.

Everyone involved in care will see the same information at the same time.

This is the kind of transparency families have been begging for, and agencies have never had the bandwidth to provide.

There will be no more:

guessing
chasing updates
misunderstandings
or crossed wires.

Visibility will replace confusion.

---

5. AI Will Standardize Quality Without Dehumanizing Care

One of the biggest challenges in home care is consistency.

Two caregivers can perform the same task in completely different ways.
Two families can receive two entirely different versions of care.
Two operators can interpret documentation differently.

AI will standardize quality by:

guiding tasks
ensuring compliance
flagging deviations
tracking performance
and measuring consistency.

This does not remove the human element.
It strengthens it.

Caregivers will still bring personality and compassion.
AI will bring predictability and structure.

For the first time, quality will no longer depend on luck, staffing, or chance.

Together, they create quality at scale.

---

6. Oversight Will Shift From Supervisory to Strategic

Supervisors today spend their time:

monitoring
correcting
chasing
coaching
documenting
triaging
and putting out fires.

AI will handle the monitoring.
Supervisors will handle the humans.

Their role will shift to:

skill building
supporting caregivers
strengthening relationships
problem solving
and improving client outcomes.

This is what supervision was supposed to be all along.
AI simply makes it possible.

Oversight will become more meaningful because supervisors will finally have time to do the work they were originally hired to do.

---

7. Families Will Finally Get the Transparency They Have Wanted for Years

Families are not asking for perfection.
They are asking for clarity.

They want to know:

what happened
when it happened
who did it
and what comes next.

AI will give families a level of transparency that the old model could never deliver.

Live updates.
Completed tasks.
Health changes.
Behavior patterns.
Risk alerts.
Daily summaries.

This transparency will rebuild trust in an industry where trust has been slipping for years.

Families will no longer feel like outsiders. They will feel informed and connected.

---

8. AI Will Make Care Safer, Not Riskier

The fear around AI always centers on risk.
But the reality is the current model is already full of risk:

missed medications
incorrect transfers
incomplete notes

missed warning signs
inconsistent training
and preventable injuries

AI reduces risk by:

improving accuracy
enhancing communication
guiding tasks
detecting problems
and providing real-time support

Care will not feel automated.
It will feel safer.

---

9. AI Will Allow Care to Scale Without Increasing Burnout

The biggest limitation in home care has always
been human capacity.
You cannot scale a system that relies entirely on
people doing everything manually.

AI will allow the industry to scale by:

reducing administrative work
automating documentation
supporting oversight
improving training
simplifying scheduling
and increasing consistency.

Scaling will no longer mean burning out the people who make care possible.

This is how the industry grows without breaking the people inside it.

---

10. This Is the Shift That Creates the AI-Assisted Care Economy

This chapter lays the foundation for the system described in the chapters ahead.

An economy built on:

intelligence
relief
support
transparency
quality
and real-time visibility

Care will become smarter and more predictable.
Caregivers will become more empowered.
Families will become more informed.
Operators will become more efficient.

The work will remain human.
The support will become intelligent.

This is the bridge to the CareFlow Framework and the new model of caregiving.

Chapter 9: The CareFlow Framework: The Architecture of the New Model

"Care fails in the gaps. The future of caregiving is defined by how few gaps remain."

The traditional home care model was built on manual flow.

Calls flow through coordinators.
Schedules flow through offices.
Documentation flows through paperwork.
Problems flow through supervisors.
Information flows through delayed updates.
Compliance flows through auditing.

Every point of flow relies on people.
And when the pressure increases, the system collapses exactly where the flow is weakest.

The next era of care will not be defined by more effort.
It will be defined by better flow.

Flow of information.
Flow of guidance.
Flow of tasks.

Flow of documentation.
Flow of communication.
Flow of support.

The CareFlow Framework is the structure that explains how the next generation of caregiving will operate.
It is not a product.
It is the map.

A map of how intelligence will move through the care moment in real time, rather than waiting for human intervention.

This chapter outlines the architecture that replaces the old model and makes scale possible.

---

1. Flow of Information: Everything Starts With Clarity

In the traditional model, information is trapped in:

binders
care plans
shift notes
voicemails
emails
and office files.

Caregivers receive outdated instructions.
Families receive partial updates.
Supervisors receive late reports.

The future of care begins with a single idea:

Information must be accurate, immediate, and shared.

In the CareFlow Framework, information flows:

from caregiver to family
from family to caregiver
from caregiver to oversight
from oversight to the entire care plan
from the care moment straight into the system

Nothing is delayed.
Nothing is hidden.
Nothing depends on the right person checking the right message at the right time.

Care demands clarity.
Flow provides it.

---

2. Flow of Guidance: Support Must Happen in the Moment

Training today is disconnected from real care.

Orientation happens before the work.
Coaching happens after mistakes.
Support happens when someone is finally available to pick up the phone.

None of this matches the urgency of the care moment.

In the CareFlow Framework, guidance flows instantly:

safe transfer cues
meal preparation reminders
dementia behavior tips
mobility support
safety protocols
medication administration rules.

Guidance becomes part of the work, not a separate task.

Caregiver confidence rises.
Client risk falls.
Consistency improves.

Support flows to the caregiver, not from them.

---

3. Flow of Documentation: Notes Must Write Themselves

Documentation has become the silent killer of home care.

Caregivers dread it.
Supervisors chase it.
Agencies depend on it.
Regulators require it.
Families never see it.

Yet everything relies on it.

In the future model, documentation flows automatically from the care moment:

tasks completed
changes observed
patterns detected
summaries produced
alerts generated
care plans updated.

Caregivers perform the work.
The system captures the work.

This is the infrastructure shift that frees the workforce from the weight that has been crushing them for years.

---

4. Flow of Communication: Everyone Sees the Same Story

Communication today is a broken relay race.

Caregivers tell coordinators.
Coordinators tell families.
Families tell nurses.
Nurses tell supervisors.
Supervisors tell caregivers.

By the time the story comes full circle, everything is partial, delayed, or misunderstood.

CareFlow strips out the middle.

Communication flows straight to the people who need it:

families receive real-time updates
caregivers receive clear direction
operators receive alerts
supervisors receive summaries.

Nothing is lost.
Nothing is delayed.
Nothing is filtered.

Care becomes a shared reality rather than a chain of interpretations.

---

5. Flow of Oversight: Supervisors Do Human Work Again

Oversight today is a game of catch-up.

Supervisors react to:

late notes
missed calls
family complaints
incomplete care plans
unseen incidents
and escalating problems.

The new model changes the direction.

Oversight flows from intelligence to supervisors, not from emergencies to supervisors.

Supervisors receive:

early warnings
performance signals
pattern detection
risk flags
training recommendations.

Their time shifts to:

coaching
supporting
problem solving
relationship building
skill development.

AI handles the monitoring.
Humans handle the humans.

---

6. Flow of Quality: Consistency Becomes the New Standard

Quality in home care is inconsistent because it depends entirely on:

who is working
who is supervising
who is coordinating
and who is available

The CareFlow Framework allows quality to flow through systems instead of luck.

Tasks are standardized.
Guidance is consistent.
Documentation is accurate.
Communication is clear.
Support is immediate.

This creates a version of quality the industry has
never been able to deliver at scale.

Not a good week.
Not a strong office.
Not a lucky caregiver match.

A predictable outcome.

---

7. Flow of Safety: Risk Drops Immediately

Most safety issues happen because someone:

did not know
did not notice
did not communicate
or did not respond in time

Safety flows differently in the new model.

Alerts fire instantly.
Changes are detected automatically.
Guidance appears at the moment of risk.
Care plans shift dynamically.
Critical information routes to the right person
immediately.

Safety becomes a flow, not a crisis.

---

8. Flow of Scale: Growth Without Burnout

The old model cannot scale because scale requires:

more coordinators
more supervisors
more oversight
more documentation
more offices.

Every new client creates new administrative weight.

In the CareFlow Framework, scale flows through intelligence rather than labor.

Workflows shrink.
Tasks simplify.
Errors drop.
Coverage improves.
Retention rises.
Costs decline.

Growth no longer crushes operators.
It elevates them.

Scale becomes a feature, not a threat.

This Is the Architecture the Industry Has Been Waiting For

CareFlow is the name for a simple truth:

Care does not need more people.
Care needs better flow.

Flow of information.
Flow of guidance.
Flow of documentation.
Flow of communication.
Flow of oversight.
Flow of quality.
Flow of safety.
Flow of scale.

This is what the industry has been missing.

This is the foundation for the model that will replace the old one.

In the next chapter, we will break apart the caregiver's role in this system and show how the new model finally gives them the support they have deserved for decades.

Chapter 10: The New Role of the Caregiver: From Worker to Supported Professional

"Caregiving has always been a profession. The only thing missing was the support that made it feel like one."

For decades, caregivers have carried the weight of a system that was not built to protect them.
They have been expected to:

perform complex care
manage heavy documentation
handle emotional labor
operate with limited guidance
navigate challenging behaviors
and keep families reassured.

All while being underpaid, undervalued, and unsupported.

The traditional model treated caregivers like labor.
The future will treat them like professionals.

In the AI-assisted care economy, caregivers become the center of the system.
Not the office.

Not the coordinator.
Not the administrator.
The caregiver.

This chapter explains how the new model elevates the caregiver role and finally gives the workforce the respect, clarity, and support it has deserved for years.

---

1. The Caregiver Becomes the Primary Interface of Care

In the old model, information flowed through the office.
Caregivers were downstream from everything:

instructions
expectations
updates
and decisions.

This created confusion and inconsistency.

In the new model, the caregiver becomes the primary interface.
They receive:

live guidance
real-time changes
safety alerts
clear task lists
and intelligent updates.

Care does not pass through a coordinator first.
It flows straight to the person delivering the care.

This returns the power to the workforce that makes the entire industry possible.

---

2. Tasks Become Clear Instead of Vague

Most caregivers today walk into a home with:

a care plan written months ago
tasks that do not match the client's current needs
and expectations that change depending on who answers the phone

In the new model, tasks become:

clear
specific
guided
and updated in real time.

Caregivers no longer guess.
They know.

Clarity reduces stress.
Clarity increases consistency.
Clarity elevates the experience for families and operators.

---

3. Training Moves From Orientation to Real-Time Coaching

Orientation training is important, but it has never been enough.

Caregivers today encounter situations they were never prepared for.
They rely on instinct because support is not available when it is needed most.

In the new model, training flows during the work itself.

Caregivers receive:

step-by-step reminders
mobility cues
behavioral guidance
nutrition prompts
dementia tips
safety instructions
and situational coaching.

Training becomes ongoing, practical, and personalized.

This is how you build a confident workforce without overwhelming them.

---

4. Documentation No Longer Steals Time From Care

Documentation has always been the silent burden of the caregiver role.

It steals time.
It creates pressure.
It forces care to compete with paperwork.

In the new model, documentation becomes automatic.

AI transforms:

tasks completed
changes observed
behaviors noted
and environmental risks

into structured, accurate documentation without additional effort from the caregiver.

The caregiver performs the care.
The system handles the notes.

This shift alone will change retention, job satisfaction, and the longevity of the workforce.

---

5. Caregivers Receive Support Instead of Blame

Under the traditional model, issues often lead to blame:

a missed task
a misunderstood instruction

a late update
a care plan mistake

Caregivers are held responsible even when the system failed them.

In the new model, support flows before blame.

If something is missed:

the system catches it
the system clarifies it
the system notifies the right people

Caregivers are no longer isolated.
They are supported.

This reduces fear, frustration, and the sense of being constantly evaluated without help.

---

6. The Caregiver Becomes Part of a Feedback Loop, Not a Forgotten Worker

Caregivers rarely receive meaningful feedback because supervisors are overwhelmed.

In the new model, feedback becomes:

continuous
accurate
helpful
and rooted in data

Caregivers will know:

what they are doing well
what needs improvement
what risks are rising
and what skills they can build.

Feedback becomes professional development, not criticism.

This elevates the role of caregiving into a measurable, respected profession.

---

7. Caregivers Gain a Level of Protection They Have Never Had

Care is emotional and unpredictable.
Caregivers often walk into the unknown without any form of protection.

AI-assisted systems help protect caregivers by:

documenting what actually happened
showing completed tasks
tracking safety risks
verifying changes
and creating a neutral record

When misunderstandings occur, facts replace assumptions.

Caregivers are protected, respected, and shielded from unnecessary blame.

8. The Role Becomes More Sustainable for the Long Term

The biggest crisis in home care is not recruitment. It is retention.

Caregivers leave because:

the work is heavy
the guidance is limited
the stress is constant
the recognition is low
and the support is inconsistent

The new model reverses every one of these factors.

AI assists with the weight.
Guidance assists with the confusion.
Documentation assists with the burden.
Feedback assists with the growth.
Transparency assists with the relationships.

This creates stability in a workforce that has been unstable for decades.

---

9. Caregivers Become Partners in Care, Not Replaceable Labor

Families trust caregivers.
Caregivers understand clients.

Caregivers build the relationships that define the entire experience.

The new model recognizes this by making the caregiver:

the center
the partner
the critical link
and the one supported by intelligent infrastructure

The industry finally shifts from seeing caregivers as labor to seeing them as the professionals who sustain the entire system.

The Future of Care Is Built Around the Workforce That Has Always Carried It

The CareFlow Framework elevates the caregiver from:

unsupported worker
to supported professional

from:

guessing
to guided

from:

isolated
to connected

from:

burdened
to empowered

This is how the next decade of caregiving will look.

Not with fewer caregivers.
With stronger ones.
Not with more paperwork.
With smarter systems.
Not with a heavier load.
With real support.

In the next chapter, we will explore how this same transformation reshapes the experience for families and gives them the clarity they have been missing for years.

Chapter 11: The New Experience for Families: Clarity Instead of Confusion

"Families do not need perfection. They need visibility."

For years, families have been forced to navigate home care with incomplete information.
They are expected to trust a process they cannot see, coordinate with an office that is overwhelmed, and understand a care plan written in language that does not match real life.

The traditional model left families:

uncertain
uninformed
anxious
and often frustrated.

Not because the caregivers failed.
Not because families were difficult.
But because the system did not give either side the information they needed.

I have spoken with countless families across different states and offices, and almost all of them described the same thing: they were not asking for more services or better marketing. They were asking for clarity.

The new model changes that.
Families move from outsiders to informed partners, supported by real-time visibility, intelligent communication, and automatic clarity.

This chapter explains how the family experience is completely transformed when care is guided by intelligence instead of being buried in paperwork and office bottlenecks.

---

1. Families No Longer Have to Guess What Happened During a Visit

Today, families depend on:

text messages
voicemail
sticky notes
and occasional office updates

They rarely know:

what was done
what was missed
what changed
or what concerns were observed.

In the new model, families receive real-time visibility into the care moment:

completed tasks
safety checks
nutrition updates
mobility assistance
medication reminders
environmental changes.

Families finally know what is happening while it is happening.

The anxiety created by uncertainty is gone.

---

2. Daily Summaries Replace Office Phone Calls

Office teams try to keep families updated, but they are stretched thin.

Updates become:

late
incomplete
inconsistent
or forgotten.

Office staff want to communicate more often, but they spend most of their day putting out fires that the system itself creates.

In the new model, daily summaries are generated automatically:

what the caregiver did
any changes observed

alerts
recommendations
upcoming needs.

Families no longer wait for updates.
Updates come to them.

This reduces tension, improves trust, and eliminates
miscommunication.

---

3. Alerts Identify Issues Before They Turn Into Emergencies

Families often discover problems too late:

urinary infections advancing
nutrition declining
mobility decreasing
confusion increasing
medication schedules slipping

Not because caregivers do not care, but because no
system connects the dots in time.

The new model changes this.

AI identifies:

changes in patterns
risks in behavior
environmental hazards
care inconsistencies
signs of decline

Families are notified before issues escalate.

This allows for early intervention instead of crisis management.

---

4. Families Become Part of the Care Plan, Not Just Observers

Care plans today feel like documents written for agencies, not families.

They are:

long
clinical
filled with jargon
and is rarely updated in real time.

Families often do not understand what is supposed to happen, which makes it impossible for them to give accurate direction or feedback.

In the new model, care plans become dynamic and understandable.

Families can see:

task lists
goals
progress
changes
and risk alerts.

They are not observers.
They are informed participants.

This strengthens communication and reduces conflict.

---

5. Families Can Finally Trust That Care Is Consistent

One of the biggest fears families have is inconsistency.

They worry that:

tasks vary
care quality shifts
expectations depend on the caregiver
and no one oversees the details

The new model creates consistency through:

guided tasks
standardized workflows
real-time accountability
and intelligent monitoring

Families no longer hope care is consistent.
They can see that it is.

Trust becomes evidence-based.

---

6. Miscommunications That Created Tension Are Eliminated

Many conflicts between families and caregivers come from:

unclear expectations
incomplete updates
incorrect assumptions
or lost information.

AI eliminates the gaps that cause these conflicts by:

delivering real-time updates
standardizing communication
clarifying tasks
and documenting changes

Families do not have to interpret anything.
They see exactly what happened.

This protects caregivers and reduces stress for everyone involved.

---

7. Families Receive Support at the Same Time Caregivers Do

Today, when a problem occurs, families are often notified after the fact.
They feel powerless because they are only brought into the situation once it has already escalated.

In the new model, support flows to everyone at the same time:

caregivers receive guidance
families receive updates
operators receive alerts

Everyone knows what is happening and what needs to be done.

Families feel included instead of blindsided.

---

8. Transparency Restores Trust in an Industry That Has Lost It

Home care has suffered from a slow erosion of trust.

Families often feel:

out of the loop
unsure about what they are paying for
concerned about missed tasks
and uncertain about safety

The new model restores trust by giving families clarity instead of promises.

They see:

the work
the changes
the patterns

the risks
the outcomes

Trust is no longer a marketing term.
Trust is a live feed of the care being delivered.

---

9. Families Gain Peace of Mind, Not More Questions

Families do not need more dashboards or
complicated tools.
They need peace of mind.

AI delivers peace through:

clarity
consistency
visibility
and proactive support

Families know what is happening.
They know what is coming.
They know their loved one is safe.

For the first time, home care feels stable rather than
uncertain.

This Is What Families Have Always Wanted

The new care experience is built on a simple truth:

Families never needed perfection.
They needed visibility.

When visibility becomes standard:

tension drops
trust rises
conflicts fade
and care improves

The next chapter will explain how this same clarity
transforms the experience of the operator and why
the office of the future looks nothing like the office
of the last twenty years.

Chapter 12: The New Role of the Operator: From Administrative Burden to Strategic Leadership

"Operators are not overwhelmed because they are weak. They are overwhelmed because the system forces them to carry work no one should be carrying."

Home care operators have spent decades trying to keep a collapsing structure upright.
They have carried the weight of:

scheduling
compliance
constant hiring
caregiver crises
family questions
documentation gaps
audits
billing
state regulations
technology overload
and unpredictable demand.

All while managing thin margins, high turnover, and nonstop emergencies.

I have lived this cycle for years. The work never stopped. The day never felt long enough.

The traditional model traps operators in the role of:

firefighter
crisis manager
scheduler
paperwork coordinator
complaint handler
and administrative catch-all

It is not sustainable.
It has never been sustainable.
And it is the reason so many operators burn out, sell, or walk away.

The new model redesigns the operator role entirely.

This chapter explains how intelligent systems relieve the administrative burden and allow operators to step into the leadership, strategy, and relationship roles they were meant to have.

---

1. Operators Shift From Reactive to Proactive Leadership

Operators today live in reaction mode.

The day starts with:

overnight issues
call-outs

family concerns
caregiver questions
and coordination failures.

By noon, half the day's energy is gone.

Every operator I have ever met has said the same thing. They do not want to work more. They want to work better.

In the new model, operators receive early alerts instead of late emergencies.

Issues are detected before they escalate.
Patterns are identified before they become problems.
Risks are surfaced before supervisors are blindsided.

Operators are finally allowed to lead instead of chasing.

---

2. Scheduling Becomes System-Supported Instead of Human-Dependent

Scheduling is the hidden chaos engine of home care.

Call-outs
traffic delays
miscommunication
availability gaps
double bookings
and abrupt changes.

These constant disruptions destroy office morale, overwhelm operators, and reduce care quality.

In the new model, scheduling becomes dynamic.

The system:

matches availability
fills gaps
clarifies openings
predicts issues
and recommends coverage

Operators oversee strategy, not scramble to survive the day.

---

3. Documentation No Longer Creates Bottlenecks

Operators spend a massive amount of time:

chasing notes
correcting errors
closing tasks
updating care plans
clarifying instructions.

Not because caregivers are incapable, but because documentation expectations and workflows are outdated.

The new model makes documentation flow automatically, which gives operators:

cleaner records
faster compliance
lower risk
less rework
and more accurate oversight

This frees office staff to focus on high-value activity instead of paperwork correction.

---

4. Operators Gain Immediate Visibility Into the Care Moment

Operators often operate blind.

They do not know:

what happened
what changed
what is slipping
or what is being missed

until a family calls or a caregiver complains.

The new model provides:

real-time updates
risk detection
task verification
behavioral patterns
and clear summaries.

Operators do not have to guess anymore.
They can see.

This enhances decision-making, staffing choices, and client outcomes.

---

5. Oversight Becomes Strategic Instead of Administrative

Traditional oversight is buried under:

training gaps
compliance issues
missed tasks
documentation problems
and surprise incidents.

Supervisors spend most of their time correcting errors instead of developing people.

The new model shifts oversight into a higher function.

Supervisors receive:

recommendations
coaching cues
performance signals
and early warnings.

This allows operators to design oversight plans that are:

proactive
targeted
and humane

Supervision becomes leadership, not cleanup.

---

6. Operator Stress Decreases as Office Efficiency Increases

Operator burnout is not caused by volume.
It is caused by:

chaotic workflows
unclear visibility
endless follow-ups
and constant rework

When administrative weight drops, operators can focus on what they do best:

problem solving
client relationships
business development
team leadership
and quality improvement

The new model protects the operator's energy.
It restores their capacity.
It brings back the feeling of control that the old model stripped away.

---

7. Operators Build Relationships Instead of Managing Chaos

In the traditional model, operators rarely have time for the work that actually builds a great agency.

They intend to:

visit clients
support caregivers
improve culture
build partnerships
develop leaders.

But their days are consumed by emergencies.

The new model gives that time back.

With fewer fires and more clarity, operators can focus on relationships instead of tasks.

This is what creates stable growth that is not dependent on constant crisis management.

---

8. Operators Become Strategic Thinkers, Not Exhausted Administrators

When operations flow smoothly, operators can finally step into the role the industry has never allowed them to fully embrace:

vision
planning
innovation
partnerships

expansion
and higher-level decision-making

This is what separates surviving operators from future operators.

The new model elevates the role from:

task manager to strategist
administrator to leader
overwhelmed coordinator to intelligent overseer

It transforms how operators work and how agencies grow.

---

9. The Office Becomes Lighter, Leaner, and More Effective

The operator of the future does not run a heavy office.

They run a lean, intelligent operation supported by systems that:

automate
predict
guide
standardize
and protect

Administrative headcount shifts from "necessary to survive" to "intentionally designed."

Operators finally have control over their infrastructure instead of being controlled by it.

This Is the Operator's Future

The new care model does not eliminate the operator.
It elevates them.

The operator moves from:

reactive to proactive
manual to intelligent
burdened to supported
overwhelmed to strategic
exhausted to effective

When the system becomes lighter, the operator becomes stronger.

This transition is not theoretical.
It is already happening in the industries closest to home care.

In the next chapter, we will turn to the objections, resistance, and excuses the industry will raise.
And we will explain, clearly and directly, why they are wrong.

Chapter 13: They Will Say This Will Not Work

"Every new system is called impossible right before it becomes inevitable."

The moment you introduce a new model for home care, the resistance begins.
Quiet at first. Then loud. Then unanimous.

Franchisors will say it.
Operators will say it.
Investors will say it.
Even people who agree with you will say it under their breath.

They will say this will not work.

Not because they truly believe that.
But because disruption threatens the comfort of the familiar.
And nothing in home care has been more familiar than the belief that innovation cannot take root here.

This chapter addresses the arguments that will be used to dismiss everything in this book.
Not to attack anyone.
But to show the difference between opinion and reality.

Before we begin, remember one thing.
Resistance is not analysis.
Resistance is fear wearing the mask of certainty.

---

1. "Technology tried to fix home care before. It never worked."

This is the first, loudest, and most predictable objection.

People repeat it like a truth.
But it is not a truth.
It is a story the industry tells itself to avoid accountability.

Technology never failed home care.
The early models were simply built in the wrong direction.

They tried to replace agencies.
They tried to commoditize caregivers.
They tried to centralize operations.
They tried to scale before proving.
They tried to force clients into unfamiliar structures.

The flaw was structural, not technological.

If you build a solution around the wrong problem, it fails by design.
That is what happened.

---

2. "The elderly do not use technology."

This is one of the most convenient myths in home care.

It has been repeated for so long that people stopped questioning it.

The truth is simpler.

Families are the primary users of care technology, not seniors.
And families today are tech literate, mobile-first, AI curious, outcome driven, and demanding transparency.

They want care updates.
They want risk alerts.
They want task confirmation.
They want clarity on what is happening in the home.
They want immediate communication.

They are not resisting innovation.
They are frustrated that they cannot get it.

Even older adults are using telehealth, remote monitoring, medication apps, and digital health portals.

The idea that seniors cannot adapt is not a reason to avoid change.
It is a reason to design technology that removes complexity instead of adding it.

Technology does not need to be advanced.
It needs to be invisible.
It needs to serve the moment.
And it needs to support the relationship between
the family and the caregiver.

The myth is old. The users are new.
The belief simply has not caught up.

---

3. "But Honor tried this. And Honor failed."

Honor will be the industry's favorite example.
It is the case study that franchisors will point to on
stage.
It is the story operators will use to validate their
skepticism.

But here is the truth:

Honor did not fail because the idea was wrong.
Honor failed because the structure was wrong.

Honor became a national agency.
Honor became a labor marketplace.
Honor became a staffing company.
Honor became a tech-enabled provider.
Honor became four different business models at
once.

They did not eliminate the administrative burden.
They simply absorbed it on a larger scale.

They still had manual scheduling.
They still had office overhead.
They still had large call centers.
They still had compliance infrastructure.
They still had centralized staffing.
They still had inconsistent quality.

They solved logistics, not the care moment.
They streamlined the business, not the experience.

The future model is not a national agency with better software.
The future model is an intelligent ecosystem that shifts work away from humans and toward systems that can carry the weight.

Honor's story does not prove that innovation cannot work.
It proves innovation will fail when it tries to preserve yesterday's structure.

---

4. "This will cost too much. Who is going to pay for it?"

The industry loves this objection because it sounds responsible.

The reality is simple.

The cost of not transforming is already higher than the cost of innovation.

Operators today are paying for turnover, burnout, rehiring, non-billable hours, manual scheduling, documentation corrections, office overload, and lost clients.

Every one of those silent costs is more expensive than an intelligent system.

An AI-supported care model will cost less than one office coordinator.
And it will deliver more accuracy, stability, and efficiency than any human department alone could sustain.

Families will pay for visibility.
Payers will pay for outcomes.
Agencies will pay for relief.

This is not a cost.
It is a correction.

The old model is expensive by nature.
The new model reduces cost by design.

---

5. "Where will this live? Who will host it?"

This concern is outdated by nearly a decade.

No one is installing servers or building on-site infrastructure.

AI-driven care systems will be cloud-hosted, HIPAA-compliant, modular, API connected, EHR-compatible, and continuously improving.

Operators do not need IT departments.
They need clarity and simplicity.

The hosting is not the challenge.
The willingness to rethink the model is.

The world moved to the cloud years ago.
Home care simply has not followed.

---

6. "This will be too complicated to manage."

This objection sounds practical, but it collapses under reality.

The current model is already more complicated than the future one.

Today's operator manages manual onboarding, manual QA, manual scheduling, manual documentation, manual compliance, and manual client updates.

Nothing about this is simple.

An intelligent care ecosystem simplifies what already exists.
It reduces steps.
It reduces risk.

It removes duplication.
It lifts the weight from offices and field staff.

AI simplifies home care.
The old model complicates it.

If complexity were the barrier, the existing structure would have collapsed decades ago.

---

7. "Caregivers will not use AI."

Caregivers already use mobile scheduling, GPS clock-ins, text instructions, training videos, apps, gig platforms, and digital onboarding.

The modern caregiver is not resisting technology. They are resisting systems that add pressure without adding support.

Give them something that lifts weight from their day, and they will embrace it immediately.

Caregivers do not need to be convinced.
They need to be helped.

Support creates adoption.
Relief creates trust.

---

8. "Families will never trust this."

Families trust whatever gives them visibility, communication, proof, and peace of mind.

They trust hospitals.
They trust telehealth.
They trust medical portals.
They trust monitoring devices.
They trust wellness apps.
They trust digital records.

The only thing families do not trust is silence.

The current home care model is built on silence.
The new model eliminates it.

Trust increases when communication increases.
This is not complicated.

Families want clarity.
The old model cannot provide it.
The new model delivers it by default.

---

9. "This threatens agencies."

This objection exposes the real fear.
Operators assume the new model will replace them.

But the new model does not eliminate the operator.
It elevates them.

It eliminates administrative burden.
It eliminates chaotic scheduling.
It eliminates documentation pressure.

It eliminates office fatigue.
It eliminates reactive leadership.
It eliminates endless rework.
It eliminates operational noise.

The operators who understand this will lead the next decade.
The ones who fear it will shrink.

AI is not competition.
AI is capacity.

---

10. "Private equity thinks this model scales."

Private equity firms buying ten or fifteen franchises at a time will push back hardest.

Their entire strategy is built on yesterday's economics:

heavy staffing
large offices
manual scheduling
predictable reimbursement
centralized compliance
labor-dependent margins

AI disrupts all of that.
It shifts power away from multi-territory conglomerates and back into smaller, lighter operations that can move faster.

The PE consolidation bubble will burst because it is tied to a model that is already collapsing.

You cannot scale a structure that is breaking.
You can only replace it.

Momentum builds from clarity, not consolidation.

---

11. "Care.com already tried this."

This objection comes from people who do not understand the difference between a directory and a care model.

Care.com is a list.
A phone book with profiles.
A marketplace without accountability.

It offers no real-time support.
No risk alerts.
No documentation.
No task verification.
No coaching.
No supervision.
No family guidance.
No quality control.

It matches people and leaves them on their own.

The future model is not a directory.
The future model is not a marketplace.
The future model is not a gig platform.

The future is an intelligent ecosystem that supports the moment of care, not the transaction.

Markets connect people.
Ecosystems support them.

---

12. "We have always done it this way."

So did Blockbuster.
So did Kodak.
So did taxis.
So did malls.
So did newspapers.
So did cable companies.

Every collapsing sector used those six words as its shield.

Home care is next unless it evolves.

The story does not end with tradition.
The story ends with transformation.

Stability is not the same as sustainability.
The industry confuses the two.

---

13. "It will not work."

This is the final objection.
The last defense.

The phrase every declining system uses to protect itself.

And yet the truth is simple.

It will not work for agencies that refuse to change.
It will not work for franchisors who refuse to innovate.
It will not work for operators who refuse to think beyond crisis management.

But for the families, caregivers, and operators who have lived the pain of the old model, something new is not a risk.

It is a necessity.

The future does not wait for permission.
The future does not ask for agreement.
The future does not negotiate with resistance.

The future arrives.
And the system either adapts or becomes irrelevant.

The world is already moving toward the AI-assisted care economy.
The industry can argue about it.
But it cannot stop it.

This is what we are stepping into.
And the ones who see it clearly will lead it.

Chapter 14: The AI-Assisted Care Model: How It Actually Works

"The future of care will not be automated. It will be amplified."

By this point in the book, one thing should be clear.

The old model cannot carry the next decade.
The workforce cannot expand fast enough.
Families cannot absorb any more pressure.
Operators cannot survive the administrative weight.

The only path forward is a model where intelligence carries what people cannot.

Not to replace the caregiver.
Not to remove the human connection.
But to remove the chaos behind it.

This is where the AI-assisted care model begins.

It does not start with robots.
It does not start with automation.
It starts with a simple belief.

Care needs to be supported, not supervised.

AI is the support.

The Three Pillars of the AI-Assisted Model

Most people imagine AI as a single tool.
In reality, it is a layered support system woven around the people doing the work.

The model has three pillars.

---

1. Intelligent Coordination

This is the backbone.
The system analyzes:

patterns
risks
scheduling shifts
client needs
caregiver availability
transportation timing
and geographic efficiency.

Not daily.
Not hourly.
In real time.

Operators are removed from administrative firefighting.
Caregivers are removed from confusion and conflicting instructions.
Families receive clarity instead of doubt.

The coordinator becomes the system.
The human becomes the relationship.

This is where the second pillar takes over.

---

2. Intelligent Support

Caregiving breaks down in the moments where people feel alone.

AI support answers that moment.

A caregiver can say:

"I am not sure what to do right now."
"I think something is changing with the client."
"I need clarity on what is expected."

And AI responds with guidance, coaching, alerts, or next steps.
Instantly.
Accurately.
Without shame.
Without delay.

This is what agencies have never been able to deliver consistently.

It turns the caregiver from an isolated worker into a supported partner.

This is where the third pillar steps in.

3. Intelligent Visibility

Families do not want more checkboxes. They want clarity.

They want to know:

What happened today.
What changed.
What needs attention.
What is improving.
What is declining.
What is normal.
What is concerning.

AI visibility creates a real-time window into the care experience.

Not pages of documentation.
Not end-of-shift summaries.
Just simple, accurate, human-centered information delivered without burden.

The family is no longer guessing.
The caregiver is no longer blamed.
The operator is no longer blind.

The Future Model Is Not a Marketplace. It Is a Support System.

People confuse AI with gig work, apps, platforms, and online directories.

This is none of that.

A marketplace connects people.
AI supports them.

A gig platform dispatches workers.
AI equips them.

A directory lists profiles.
AI guides care.

This model is not replacing the structure of home care.
It is replacing the weight of it.

Everything that makes agencies overwhelmed becomes infrastructure.
Everything that makes caregiving difficult becomes supported.
Everything that makes families anxious becomes visible.

This is not theory.
This is the only version of home care that can survive the next wave of demand.

What This Looks Like in Practice

The model works like this:

A caregiver clocks in.
The system analyzes historical notes, client health indicators, previous tasks, risks, and caregiver strengths.

Within seconds, it provides suggestions, reminders, and guidance tailored to that specific shift.

If something changes, the system flags it.
If something improves, the system documents it.
If something risks harm, the system alerts it.

The operator is notified only when necessary.
The family receives insight only when helpful.
The caregiver receives support the entire time.

The model removes friction, not people.
It replaces pressure, not relationships.
It strengthens the care moment instead of complicating it.

Why This Works

This works because care is pattern-based.
Risk is pattern-based.
Human behavior is pattern-based.
Decline is pattern-based.
Caregiver burnout is pattern-based.
Missed shifts are pattern-based.

AI sees patterns that humans cannot.
And it does it instantly.

This is why the next generation of home care will be defined by intelligence.

Not because AI is powerful.

But because the people who care deserve better support than the old model can give them.

This Is Not the End of Human Care. It Is the Beginning of Better Care.

The goal has never been to remove the human.
The goal is to remove the weight wrapped around the human.

Home care was never broken because the caregivers were wrong.
It was broken because the structure was.

This model restores the relationship that matters most:
the caregiver and the client.

And it surrounds them with a layer of intelligence that ensures the work becomes lighter, safer, and more sustainable.

This is the future of care.
A model that lifts instead of drains.
A model that supports instead of supervises.
A model that finally fits the world we live in.

This chapter is not a forecast.
It is a framework.
And the chapters ahead explain how this model becomes real.

Chapter 15: Why Intelligence, Not Infrastructure, Will Define the Next Era of Home Care

"Systems fail when they rely on people to carry what only intelligence can hold."

For as long as home care has existed, growth has been tied to infrastructure.

More caregivers.
More schedulers.
More office staff.
More administrators.
More managers.
More layers.
More paperwork.
More oversight.

The assumption has always been simple.
If you want to grow, you must add more people who solve more problems with more effort.

But the next era of home care will not be built on effort.
It will be built on intelligence.

Not intelligence that replaces people.
Intelligence that absorbs the weight they were
never supposed to carry.

Bandwidth limited the Old Model

Every crisis in home care reveals the same truth.

People are doing work that no human can sustain.

responding to every shift change
processing last-minute cancellations
managing unpredictable needs
coordinating caregivers with imperfect information
tracking documentation across multiple systems
predicting decline without real data
communicating with families under stress
solving problems without context

A human coordinator can only carry so much.
A caregiver can only guess so much.
A family can only wait so long.
An operator can only be pulled in so many
directions.

The system collapses when the demands exceed
the attention available.

And today, everything exceeds attention.

Demand.
Turnover.

Documentation.
Risk.
Expectations.
Complexity.

Infrastructure cannot solve this.
Intelligence can.

This is the first truth the industry must confront.

The Next Era Will Not Be Built on Offices or Staff Size

Agencies used to measure strength by the size of their infrastructure.

A bigger office meant stability.
A larger staff meant reach.
More coordinators meant more control.
More managers meant more consistency.

That made sense twenty years ago.
It does not make sense now.

The future winners will not be the agencies with the biggest back office.
It will be the agencies with the smallest one.

Not because smaller is cheaper.
But because smaller is smarter.

Intelligent systems carry out tasks that used to require:

a full-time scheduler
a quality assurance department
a care manager
a weekend coordinator
a triage team
a training supervisor

The next era of home care is not a race to build.
It is a race to unburden.

This leads to the next truth the industry has avoided.

Infrastructure Grows in Cost. Intelligence Grows in Capability.

This is the shift the industry has not prepared for.

Infrastructure grows more expensive over time.
AI grows more capable over time.

Infrastructure struggles to scale.
AI scales instantly.

Infrastructure breaks under pressure.
AI adapts under pressure.

Infrastructure needs supervision.
AI provides supervision.

This is why the future cannot be built on the old structure.
The economics no longer work.

The margins no longer support it.
The workforce no longer fits it.
The expectations no longer align with it.

We are moving from a labor-based model to an intelligence-supported model.
Not to replace labor.
To protect it.

The shift becomes even clearer through one lens.

Why Intelligence Wins

There are five reasons intelligence wins over infrastructure.

1. Intelligence removes friction

Every point of friction in home care is caused by incomplete information.

Late arrivals.
Missed updates.
Confusing expectations.
Unclear tasks.
Poor handoffs.
Gaps between shifts.
Miscommunication between offices and families.

AI solves friction because it eliminates guessing.

2. Intelligence reduces risk

Most decline is predictable.
Most emergencies have early indicators.
Most safety issues show patterns.

Humans do not have the time or awareness to see it.
AI does.

3. Intelligence creates consistency

Humans vary.
Systems do not.

Every caregiver gets the same support.
Every family receives the same clarity.
Every operator gains the same insight.

Consistency is not the enemy of compassion.
It is what protects it.

4. Intelligence scales instantly

A human team has limits.
A system does not.

Scaling with people is linear.
Scaling with intelligence is exponential.

5. Intelligence protects the people who do the work

Home care does not collapse because caregivers stop caring.
It collapses because they are alone.

AI turns isolation into support.
Stress into stability.
Pressure into partnership.

The case for intelligence is not emotional. It is structural.

Three Questions define the Future Will

When people look back on this moment a decade from now, they will ask three questions.

1. Who could see the shift coming

The ones who understood that infrastructure was aging faster than the population.

2. Who adapted first

The ones who restructured their operations around patterns instead of panic.

3. Who built for intelligence instead of expansion

The ones who realized that more offices, more staff, and more layers were not the answer.

The future of home care will belong to the operators who choose intelligence now, not later.

And that leads to the most important truth of all.

The Model That Wins Is the Model That Thinks

Care cannot wait for a callback.
Care cannot wait for a scheduler.
Care cannot wait for office hours.
Care cannot wait for a weekly check-in.

The model that wins is the model that thinks in real time.

The model that sees risks before they happen.
The model that supports caregivers the moment they need help.
The model that keeps families informed without overwhelming them.
The model that keeps operators out of constant crisis management.

The model that carries what humans cannot.

This is why the future is not infrastructure.
It is intelligence.

And the operators who embrace this will build the version of home care the industry should have built years ago.

This chapter is not a forecast. It is a framework. And the chapters ahead explain how this model becomes real.

Chapter 16: What Caregivers Will Gain in the AI-Assisted Care Economy

"Caregivers were never the weakness in the system. They were the weight bearers."

If there is one truth the industry has ignored for too long, it is this:

Caregivers did not cause the collapse.
Caregivers carried it as long as they could.

The workloads.
The confusion.
The documentation.
The constant call-outs.
The emotional labor.
The unpredictable shifts.

The system survived because caregivers tolerated what the model demanded.
But tolerance is not sustainability.

The AI-assisted care economy does not replace caregivers.
It restores them.

It gives back what the old model took.

---

1. Caregivers Gain Clarity Instead of Guessing

Most caregiver stress does not come from the work.
It comes from uncertainty.

Not knowing what the family expects.
Not knowing what changes matter.
Not knowing what the office wants documented.
Not knowing when to call for help.
Not knowing if they are doing enough.
Not knowing if they will be blamed when
something goes wrong.

AI turns guessing into guidance.

The caregiver receives:

clear tasks.
clear reminders.
clear expectations.
clear updates.
clear support.
clear next steps.

They no longer walk into a shift hoping they have
the right information.
They walk in prepared.

Clarity creates confidence.
Confidence creates better care.

---

2. Caregivers Gain Support Instead of Isolation

The biggest emotional burden in home care is not the work.
It is feeling alone while doing it.

A caregiver in a home is often:

the nurse
the companion
the housekeeper
the observer
the crisis manager
the emotional support
the historian
the communicator

And they do all of this without backup.

AI gives caregivers real-time support in the moments they used to face alone.

A caregiver can ask:

What should I do next?
Is this normal?
How do I document this?
Does this need to be escalated?
What is the care plan expecting?

And instead of waiting on hold or hoping someone answers, they get immediate guidance.

Support creates stability.
Stability creates retention.

3. Caregivers Gain Protection Instead of Blame

Caregivers often absorb responsibility for problems that were never theirs.

Families blame them.
Agencies blame them.
Systems blame them.
Surveys blame them.
Documentation gaps blame them.

AI creates transparency that protects caregivers from unfair blame.

The system shows:

what was done
what was requested
what changed
what time tasks occurred
what alerts were triggered
what instructions were given.

This is not surveillance.
This is protection.

It protects caregivers from inaccurate assumptions.
It protects families from uncertainty.
It protects agencies from liability.

Transparency protects everyone.

4. Caregivers Gain Predictability Instead of Chaos

The current model is reactive.
Schedules change constantly.
Shift details change at the last minute.
Tasks shift without warning.
Client needs escalate without preparation.

AI stabilizes the day.

It predicts risks.
It anticipates needs.
It flags changes early.
It updates the care plan instantly.
It removes unnecessary surprises.

Caregivers can finally plan their day instead of surviving it.

Predictability reduces burnout.
Burnout is the real enemy.

---

5. Caregivers Gain Better Matching Instead of Random Assignments

Most caregivers are matched by:

who is closest
who is available
who is not already burnt out
who answers the phone

AI matches based on:

skills
personality
experience level
patterns
preferences
client needs
historical outcomes

Caregivers are placed where they perform best.
Not where the office is desperate.

This lifts performance.
This lifts morale.
This lifts the entire care experience.

---

6. Caregivers Gain Progress Instead of Plateaus

The old model does not create career paths.
It creates cycles.

Caregivers go case to case, shift to shift, home to home, with little recognition or development.

AI changes the dynamic.

Every shift becomes:

data
patterns
insight
strengths
growth opportunities

Caregivers finally receive feedback that helps them improve.

Not criticism.
Not blame.
Actual development.

This opens the door for:

advanced roles
specialization
mentorship opportunities
higher-tier assignments
rewarded expertise.

Caregivers become professionals with a pathway.
Not just bodies filling gaps.

---

7. Caregivers Gain Time Instead of Tasks

AI removes the administrative weight that steals time from caregiving.

Caregivers spend more time with the client.
Less time wrestling with paperwork.
Less time figuring out documentation.
Less time chasing the office.
Less time repeating information.
Less time explaining themselves.

Time is the real currency.

Caregivers gain time by giving up nothing.
The system carries the load they never should have carried.

---

8. Caregivers Gain Voice Instead of Silence

In the old model, no one asks the caregiver what they see.

But caregivers see everything.

They notice the decline before the family does.
They notice changes before the nurse does.
They notice patterns before the agency does.
They notice risks before anyone else does.

AI gives caregivers a structured way to be heard.

Their observations become data.
Their experiences become insight.
Their instincts become part of the system.

The caregiver becomes a source of intelligence.
Not just labor.

The Future Does Not Replace the Caregiver. It Respects Them.

The narrative that AI replaces people exists only in industries that misunderstand the work.

Home care is not one of those industries.

Caregivers are irreplaceable.
Caregivers are the heart.
Caregivers are the relationship.
Caregivers are the difference between safety and fear.
Caregivers are the backbone of the entire care economy.

The only thing that needs replacing is the weight they carry.

The AI-assisted care economy does not erase the caregiver.
It restores them.
It strengthens them.
It protects them.
It amplifies them.

The future of home care will belong to caregivers who are supported, not those who are stretched beyond their limits.

And this time, the system will finally be built around the people who have carried it all along.

Chapter 17: The AI-Supported Caregiver

"Caregivers do not need more pressure. They need more support."

Before we talk about the technology, the intelligence layer, the automation, or the ecosystem, we have to talk about the heart of this entire model.

The caregiver.

Caregivers have been asked to hold up a collapsing structure for years.

They have carried the weight of:

documentation
last-minute schedule changes
unsafe homes
unseen risks
overwhelming expectations
inconsistent training
and families who are desperate for reassurance

And they have done all of it with limited support.

The AI-assisted care economy is not designed to replace caregivers.
It is designed to protect them.

It is designed to give them breathing room.
It is designed to give them clarity.
It is designed to strengthen the work they already do.
It is designed to remove the weight that pushes them out of the industry.

This chapter is not about technology.

This chapter is about the caregiver's future.

---

1. The New Role of the Caregiver

In the old model, caregivers were expected to:

guess
remember
problem solve without context
document without tools
communicate without support
and carry the entire burden of the day.

In the new model, caregivers become:

supported
informed
guided
protected
and elevated.

The work does not become heavier.
The work becomes safer and clearer.

When a caregiver enters a shift, they are not walking into uncertainty.
They are walking into structured support.

---

2. Real-Time Guidance That Protects Caregivers, Not Monitors Them

This is one of the biggest misunderstandings about AI in home care.

Intelligence is not surveillance.
Intelligence is support.

It clarifies the next best step.
It highlights risks before they become emergencies.
It helps caregivers document the day without writing novels.
It gives them insight into changes they might have missed.
It backs them when families question the day.

The caregiver is no longer alone in the moment of care.
The system stands beside them.

---

3. The Shift From Reactive to Proactive Care

Caregivers have always been expected to catch changes early.

The irony is that the system made it nearly impossible for them to do so.

AI changes that.

The new model helps caregivers see:

patterns
behavioral shifts
nutrition concerns
mobility changes
mood variations
daily rhythms

before they escalate.

Care becomes proactive rather than reactive.

This reduces stress, confusion, and the sense of constant crisis management.

A supported caregiver is a confident caregiver.
A confident caregiver stays in the industry.

---

4. Training That Actually Fits the Reality of the Job

Traditional training is:

generic
outdated
inconsistent
and disconnected from the home.

The new model provides:

micro training
short targeted lessons
scenario-based modules
voice-guided instructions
real-time reinforcement.

Training becomes something caregivers use, not
something they endure.

Their skills grow with their cases.
Their confidence grows with their experience.
Their stability grows with their support.

Training stops being a checkbox.
It becomes a tool.

---

5. Caregivers Gain Freedom Instead of Losing It

The fear operators have is that AI will "control"
caregivers.

The reality is the opposite.

AI removes the pressure that steals their autonomy.

Caregivers gain freedom because they no longer
have to:

guess what the care plan is when the office forgets
to update it
wait for someone to answer the phone

figure out what to do when something changes
stress over unclear instructions
wonder if the family will be upset
take on tasks they were never trained for
hold responsibility without support.

Freedom comes from clarity.
Clarity comes from intelligence.

---

6. Documentation Becomes Effortless

Documentation is one of the most stressful parts of the job.

Agencies demand it.
Families want it.
Payers require it.
But caregivers do not have time to create it.

AI changes the workflow entirely.

Documentation becomes:

guided
automated
smart
simplified.

Caregivers speak or tap.
The system captures and organizes.

They no longer carry the mental burden of remembering every detail at the end of a long day.

The system remembers for them.

---

7. Safety Becomes Shared Instead of Personal

Today, when a client falls, declines, stops eating, or shows signs of confusion, caregivers feel responsible for missing it.

But caregivers should never be the only line of defense.

AI distributes responsibility.

It sees patterns.
It flags changes.
It triggers alerts.
It clarifies risks.
It recommends interventions.
It notifies families or operators.

Caregivers become supported humans, not stressed-out safety nets.

When the system helps protect them, caregivers stay longer and work stronger.

---

8. Respect Finally Becomes Structural

The industry has always said caregivers deserve respect.

But respect is not a slogan.
Respect is structure.

Respect is:

technology that makes their job easier
systems that do not overload them
training that meets them where they are
support that shows up every time
tools that anticipate their needs.

AI does not replace respect.
AI gives the industry a way to deliver it.

Caregivers deserve the best tools.
They have never had them.

This model changes that.

The Caregiver Is the Center. AI Is the Support. The System Is the Problem.

The story of home care has been wrong for years.

The problem was never the caregiver.
It was the system around them.

The solution is not replacing caregivers.
It is replacing the structure that overwhelms them.

The AI-supported caregiver is not science fiction.
It is the next chapter of caregiving.

A supported caregiver stays.
A supported caregiver thrives.
A supported caregiver protects families.
A supported caregiver becomes the foundation of the next decade.

The future of home care begins with the people who make home care possible.

Everything else is infrastructure.

Chapter 18: The AI-Supported Family

"Families stop panicking when they stop guessing."

If caregivers are the heart of home care, families are the nervous system.

They feel every shift.
Every silence.
Every unanswered call.
Every late update.
Every moment when something does not feel right.

For years, families have been carrying an invisible burden that the system has never acknowledged.

The worry.
The guilt.
The confusion.
The lack of clarity.
The constant questioning.
The fear that something might happen when they are not there.

Traditional home care never solved this problem.
It managed around it.

The AI-supported care model solves it directly.

This chapter is not about replacing human reassurance.
It is about giving families what they have never had:

a clear view of what is happening in the home.

---

1. Families Want Information, Not Perfection

Most operators misunderstand families.

Families do not expect:

perfect caregivers
perfect days
perfect outcomes
perfect communication.

Families expect:

honesty
visibility
consistency
and a sense of control.

They want to know if the care is happening.
They want to know that the small things are not being ignored.
They want to know someone is watching the patterns.
They want to know the caregiver is supported.
They want to know they will be notified before a small issue becomes a crisis.

When you give families clarity, trust grows automatically.

---

2. The New Family Experience Begins With Visibility

The traditional model forces families to guess.

Has mom eaten?
How was her mood today?
Did she sleep?
Did she take her medication?
Has she been showering?
Did the caregiver arrive on time?
Was anything different today?

Families should not need to call the office to answer questions about the person they love.

The new model gives families:

real-time updates
completed tasks
mood and mobility notes
meal tracking
hydration logging
risk alerts
care plan changes
and shift summaries.

They do not need long reports.
They need simple clarity.

AI shapes that clarity automatically.

---

3. Families Become Partners Instead of Outsiders

In the old model, families were observers.
In the new model, families become partners.

They gain:

guidance
recommendations
context
risk explanations
pattern insights
and clear next steps.

The system does not overwhelm them.
It simplifies decisions.

When something changes, families know:

what happened
why it matters
what to do
and who to contact.

Families make better decisions because the system
gives them better information.

---

4. Peace of Mind Comes From Predictability, Not Promises

Families are anxious because home care is unpredictable.

Caregivers change.
Schedules change.
Conditions change.
Unexpected events happen.

AI cannot erase uncertainty.
But it can structure it.

It can detect a change early.
It can notify automatically.
It can create routines.
It can stabilize the day.
It can reduce surprises.

Peace of mind does not come from saying everything is fine.
Peace of mind comes from proving it.

---

5. Families Get Answers Before They Form Questions

The strongest value intelligence provides to families is anticipation.

The system sees patterns that families cannot see.

Eating less than usual
More nighttime bathroom trips
Increased confusion in the evening

Shorter walking distance
Difficulty following instructions
Changes in tone
Changes in routine.

Families are notified early instead of being notified late.

They do not have to wonder what changed.
They do not have to guess if something is wrong.
They do not have to wait until the next doctor's appointment.

The system speaks before the problem grows.

---

6. The Biggest Pain Point of Families Finally Disappears

One of the most common complaints in home care is simple:

"No one told me."

No one told me Mom was getting weaker.
No one told me she was not eating.
No one told me she was not showering.
No one told me Dad was wandering.
No one told me he was refusing medication.
No one told me things were getting worse.

It is not the event that breaks trust.
It is the surprise.

AI removes the surprise.

Families get a steady flow of small, clear signals instead of sudden emergencies.

Communication becomes a constant, not a crisis response.

---

7. Families Feel Safer Because Caregivers Feel Supported

When caregivers are overwhelmed, families feel it immediately.

Late tasks.
Incomplete notes.
Missed details.
Rushed shifts.
Confusion about instructions.

Families know when a caregiver is sinking.

When caregivers are supported, families feel it just as fast.

More consistency.
More accuracy.
More calm.
More confidence.

Caregivers who feel supported create families who feel safe.

The AI-supported model aligns the interests of both.

---

8. The Family Experience Finally Matches the Modern World

Families manage every other part of life through technology:

banking
prescriptions
appointments
travel
communication
health records
notifications
real-time updates.

Home care has been the only area of life still operating in the dark.

The new model ends the blackout.

Families get an experience that feels modern, familiar, intuitive, and trustworthy.

They do not need training.
They do not need onboarding.
They do not need to learn new habits.

The model fits the world they already live in.

---

9. Family Stress Drops. Family Confidence Rises. Family Outcomes Improve.

When families know what is happening, they stop fearing the worst.

Stress drops.
Engagement increases.
Decision-making improves.
Conversations with caregivers become clearer.
Support systems activate earlier.
Hospitalizations decrease.
Care plans stabilize.

This is not optimism.
This is pattern-driven reality.

Visibility changes everything.

This Is the Family Experience the Old Model Could Never Deliver

Traditional home care tried to fix family anxiety with:

reassurance
phone calls
paper notes
periodic updates
manual check-ins.

It reduced fear temporarily but never eliminated it.

The AI-supported model does not try to convince families that everything is fine.
It shows them.

The difference is everything.

Chapter 19: What the New Day Looks Like

"The future is not a theory. It is a workflow."

To understand the AI-assisted care economy, you cannot think conceptually.
You have to see it.
You have to feel it.
You have to step inside a single day and experience how the model functions in real life.

This chapter is not exaggeration.
It is not science fiction.
It is not an unrealistic guess.

Everything described here already exists in pieces. The future is the moment those pieces finally work together.

This is what a single day looks like inside the new system.

---

1. The Morning Scan

Before the caregiver arrives, the system already knows what the day should look like.

It reviews:

sleep patterns
overnight movement
meal consistency
medication timing
risk flags
behavioral trends
and mobility patterns.

If anything has changed from the norm, the system highlights it.

A gentle notification goes to the caregiver before the shift starts.

"Client woke up three times last night."
"Client ate less yesterday than usual."
"Client showed decreased steps over the past two days."

The caregiver walks in prepared instead of guessing.

The family receives the same information without needing to ask.

No panic.
No confusion.
Just context.

---

2. The Arrival

The caregiver checks in through their phone.
The system verifies location, time, and schedule.

But something deeper happens in the new model.

The moment the caregiver arrives, the system automatically loads today's care priorities.
Not based on generic tasks.
Based on real data.

If hydration was low yesterday, hydration gets prioritized.
If fall risk increases, mobility support gets highlighted.
If the mood is low, engagement gets added.

The care plan evolves with the person.
Not with paperwork.

---

3. The Morning Rhythm

The caregiver starts the morning routine, but with support.

As they move through tasks, the system quietly works in the background.

It listens.
It observes trends.
It simplifies documentation.
It recognizes patterns.
It creates summaries in real time.

The caregiver taps a button.
"Breakfast prepared."

"Medication taken."
"Morning hygiene complete."

The system fills in the details.

The caregiver is not writing notes at the end of the day.
The notes write themselves.

---

4. The Midday Insight

Halfway through the shift, the system does a quick scan.

If appetite is lower than usual, it notifies the caregiver.
If mobility is different, the system suggests a light exercise routine.
If the mood is unusual, it prompts the caregiver to engage the client.

Families get real-time updates.
Not constant noise.
Just the moments that matter.

"Your mother ate less than usual but is hydrated."
"Your father walked farther today than yesterday."
"Your mother is in good spirits this morning."

Small signals create big peace of mind.

---

5. The Afternoon Course Correction

Care is rarely predictable.
Something always changes.

A new prescription.
A missed phone call.
A family request.
A sudden mood shift.
A small hazard in the home.

Traditional home care forces caregivers to figure it out alone.

The new model adjusts automatically.

If a change occurs, the system updates the rest of the day:

tasks shift
priorities reorder
alerts trigger
tips appear
documentation adjusts
family notifications update

Everything stays aligned.

Chaos gets replaced with clarity.

---

6. The Evening Check Out

At the end of the shift, the caregiver completes a simple closing routine.

They tap a few confirmations.
The system compiles the entire day:

tasks completed
hydration levels
mobility trends
mood notes
nutrition variations
medication timing
safety observations
patterns
risks
changes.

The caregiver does not write the summary.
The system does.

It delivers it to the family.
It files it for the operator.
It logs it for compliance.

There is no backlog.
No messy paperwork.
No incomplete notes.

The caregiver leaves with peace.
The family ends the day informed.
The operator ends the day prepared.

---

7. Overnight Monitoring Without Surveillance

When the caregiver leaves, the system continues to track simple patterns.

No cameras.
No invasiveness.
No monitoring that replaces human presence.

Just pattern recognition through:

motion sensors
sleep data
medication timing
bathroom activity
and environmental cues.

Families get notified if something changes.
Operators get notified when something needs attention.
Caregivers get notified when their next shift requires adjustments.

Everyone rests because the system is awake.

---

8. The Operator's View

In the old model, operators open their dashboards and feel overwhelmed.

Today's dashboard is different.

It shows:

which clients need attention
which caregivers need support
which families are concerned
which risks are rising
which outcomes improved
which tasks were completed
which patterns shifted
which problems were prevented.

Instead of reacting all day, operators see the day before it happens.

They lead with foresight, not fire drills.

The New Day Is Not About Technology

The new day is about clarity.

Caregivers are supported.
Families are informed.
Operators are prepared.
Documentation is done.
Risks are spotted early.
Tasks adapt in real time.
The home becomes safer.

The new model does not replace people.
It replaces guessing.

It replaces anxiety.
It replaces complexity.
It replaces silence.

This is what the next decade of caregiving will feel like.

Less stress.
More stability.
More dignity.
More peace.

The future is not distant.

The future is a better day.

One day at a time.

Chapter 20: Why Agencies Will Still Exist

"Intelligence does not replace leadership. It replaces chaos."

Every time a new model enters an industry, people rush to announce the end of something.

The end of taxis.
The end of bookstores.
The end of newspapers.
The end of travel agents.
The end of offices.

They say the same thing about home care.

"If AI supports caregivers directly, agencies will disappear."

That is not true.

Bad agencies will disappear.
Outdated agencies will disappear.
Operators who refuse to adapt will disappear.

But agencies as a whole will not.

The new model does not erase the operator.
It evolves the operator.

This chapter explains exactly why.

1. Families Will Always Need Oversight

Families do not want to manage the full care process alone.

They want visibility.
They want clarity.
They want communication.

But they also want someone who can:

interpret patterns
guide decisions
coordinate services
manage safety escalation
handle complex care needs
navigate policy and payer rules
support both sides in difficult moments.

AI can support the day.
It cannot replace judgment.

Agencies remain the stabilizing force between:

data
caregivers
families
payers
and outcomes.

Oversight is not going away.
It is becoming more important.

2. AI Solves Weight, Not Leadership

Home care agencies do not collapse because of a lack of leadership.

They collapse because of:

paperwork
manual scheduling
phone overload
documentation gaps
recruiting pressure
reactive planning
and staff fatigue.

AI removes the weight that has trapped operators inside crisis management.

But AI does not:

coach families
address conflict
manage compliance
support emergencies
navigate interpersonal dynamics
or handle the emotional reality of care.

Leadership is not optional.
Leadership becomes clearer when the noise is gone.

3. Escalation Will Always Need Humans

No matter how advanced the system becomes, there will always be moments when human leadership is required.

Falls
medical changes
behavioral shifts
family conflict
caregiver stress
unexpected events.

AI can detect these moments early.
AI can provide context.
AI can recommend first steps.
AI can notify all parties.

But escalation requires a human anchor.

Agencies remain that anchor.

---

4. Caregivers Still Need Human Support

Even the best system cannot replace the stability of a supportive operator.

Caregivers need:

reassurance
coaching
feedback
conflict resolution
emotional support

professional development
and someone to call when the day is heavy.

AI can lighten the load.
Agencies carry the human side.

Supported caregivers stay longer.
Operators remain essential to that support.

---

5. Agencies Become Smaller, Smarter, and More Valuable

The truth most franchisors and operators are not ready to admit is simple:

The future agency will be smaller.

Not in impact.
In structure.

A modern agency will operate with:

fewer coordinators
fewer administrative staff
lighter overhead
stronger systems
faster decision making
and a more predictable day.

The new agency is not a staffing factory.
It is an intelligence-anchored care organization.

This shift does not weaken operators.
It liberates them.

---

6. Intelligence Creates a New Competitive Landscape

Today, agencies compete on:

recruiting
staffing
response time
customer service
scheduling
and pricing.

In the future, agencies will compete on:

risk reduction
predictive care
family experience
ease of communication
documentation accuracy
care consistency
and caregiver stability.

The agencies that embrace intelligence win.
The ones that ignore it get priced out.

This is not theory.
This is market logic.

---

7. The Strongest Operators Become Care Architects

The biggest agencies will not dominate the next decade of home care.

It will be dominated by the agencies that can:

interpret data
design care workflows
anticipate needs
prevent decline
manage transitions
and support independent caregivers with structure.

Agencies transform from administrators into architects.

This is where the real value sits.

---

8. Families Will Pay for Leadership, Not Logistics

The old model forced agencies to sell:

hours
shifts
coverage
and availability.

The new model allows agencies to sell:

outcomes
stability

safety
clarity
peace of mind
coaching
and expertise.

Families will always pay for leadership they can trust.

Agencies provide that leadership.

---

9. AI Removes the Problems That Replaceable Operators Hid Behind

The operators who lose sleep every week will finally get relief.
The operators who avoided innovation will finally get exposed.

AI does not threaten strong agencies.
AI exposes the weak ones.

The operator who knows how to lead, communicate, support, and stabilize will rise.

Leadership becomes the differentiator.

Not paperwork.
Not size.
Not branding.
Not territory.

Just leadership.

The Agency Does Not Disappear. The Agency Finally Becomes What It Was Always Supposed to Be.

A partner.
A guide.
A stabilizer.
A coach.
A leader.

The agency of the future does not carry unnecessary weight.

The agency of the future carries families.

AI is not the end of the operator.

AI is the end of the operator's exhaustion.

What remains is the part of the job that always mattered.

Judgment.
Support.
Leadership.
Care.

Agencies will still exist.
But only the right ones.

Chapter 21: What Families Will Pay For Now

"Families do not pay for hours. They pay for certainty."

The biggest misunderstanding in home care is how families make decisions.

Agencies believe families buy:

hours
coverage
schedules
availability
and companionship.

Families do not buy any of that.

Families buy peace of mind.
Families buy clarity.
Families buy trust.
Families buy stability.
Families buy outcomes.

Hours are just the container.
The value is everything inside the container.

This chapter explains exactly what families will pay for in the AI-supported care economy and why traditional agencies are not structured to deliver it.

1. Families Will Pay for Visibility

The number one frustration families express is simple.

"I do not know what is happening."

They do not need long reports.
They do not need complicated dashboards.
They do not need more phone calls.

They want a clear view of:

tasks completed
medication adherence
mobility patterns
hydration
nutrition
mood
safety changes
and day-to-day trends.

Visibility is not a luxury.
Visibility is a product.

And families will pay for it every single month because it removes fear.

---

2. Families Will Pay for Early Detection

Families do not fear the present.
They fear the future.

They fear:

falls
hospitalizations
decline
wandering
medication errors
behavioral shifts
and emergencies.

AI changes the risk curve.

It detects changes early.
It identifies patterns.
It flags concerns.
It guides decisions.

The caregiver sees it.
The family sees it.
The operator sees it.

Early detection prevents crisis.
Crisis is what destroys trust.

Families will pay to avoid crisis.

---

3. Families Will Pay for Predictability

Families do not want perfection.

They want predictability.

They want:

consistent updates
consistent tasks
consistent communication
consistent caregivers
consistent routines
consistent outcomes.

Predictability reduces:

worry
panic
confusion
and the emotional weight families carry every day.

A predictable system is more valuable than a perfect system.

Families pay for what they can count on.

---

4. Families Will Pay for Communication That Makes Sense

What families hate most is silence.

The old model delivered:

sporadic updates
late notifications
generic notes

rushed calls
and unclear explanations.

The new model delivers:

simple summaries
real-time signals
short alerts
behavior notes
priority updates.

This is not more communication.
This is better communication.

Families pay for clarity.
Clarity is the new service.

---

5. Families Will Pay for Proof

The traditional home care model relied on trust
without evidence.

The new model provides trust with evidence.

Families get:

task verification
trend charts
hydration and nutrition patterns
mobility shifts
mood observations
completed routines
and documented care moments.

Families do not want to guess.
They want to see.

Proof is value.
Value is what families pay for.

---

6. Families Will Pay for Safety That Does Not Depend on Luck

Today, most safety outcomes depend on:

the right caregiver
the right day
the right moment
the right awareness.

That is luck.

Luck is not a care plan.

AI-supported safety removes luck from the equation.

Families will pay for anything that reduces the chance of hospitalization or decline.

Safety is the most valuable product in home care.
Agencies have never been able to package it.
The new model can.

---

7. Families Will Pay for a Care Team That Does Not Burn Out

Families feel the instability of agencies.

They know when caregivers are overwhelmed.
They know when offices are short-staffed.
They know when calls go unanswered.
They know when turnover is high.

They feel the chaos.

When caregivers are supported by AI, everything becomes calmer:

more accuracy
more consistency
more confidence
less guesswork
less pressure
less emotional fatigue.

Families will pay for a care environment that is stable.

Support creates stability.
Stability creates trust.
Trust creates value.

---

8. Families Will Pay for Relief, Not More Responsibility

Families already manage:

doctors
medications
appointments
insurance
prescriptions
siblings
work
their own stress.

They do not want another system they must supervise.

They want:

guidance
direction
explanations
decision support
and peace.

AI provides the invisible layer of relief.

Relief is what families pay for more than anything else.

---

9. Families Will Pay for a System That Reduces Their Mental Load

Home care today forces families to hold a mental checklist in their minds every day.

"Did she eat?"
"Did he take his meds?"
"Did she sleep?"
"Is he declining?"
"Is something wrong?"
"Should I be worried?"

Mental load is invisible, but it is heavy.

The new model carries that weight for them.

Families pay for lightness.
They pay for space.
They pay for breathing room.

This is the emotional product the old model could never deliver.

The Value Is Not the Hours. The Value Is the Experience.

Families have always paid for one thing:

the feeling that the person they love is safe.

The old model forced them to buy hours because it had nothing else to offer.

The new model gives families what they were always trying to buy:

visibility
predictability

safety
clarity
proof
relief.

This is the new value stack of home care.

Families will not hesitate to pay for it.
Because uncertainty is expensive.
And peace of mind is priceless.

Chapter 22: Where Agencies Will Lose If They Refuse to Change

"The cost of staying the same is now greater than the cost of transforming."

Every industry reaches a point where refusal becomes more expensive than adaptation.

Taxis reached that point.
Retail reached that point.
Travel agencies reached that point.
Cable reached that point.

Home care is standing at that same threshold.

The warning signs are everywhere, but many agencies are still hoping the old model can survive if they just hold on long enough.

It cannot.
Not because operators lack effort.
Not because caregivers lack dedication.
Not because families lack patience.

The old model cannot survive because the economics that held it together have already shifted.

This chapter explains exactly where agencies lose when they refuse to evolve.

---

1. Agencies Lose When They Keep Carrying Administrative Weight

Agencies today are drowning in tasks that AI can handle:

scheduling
documentation
care plan updates
family communication
shift summaries
recruiting workflows
office coordination.

Operators who refuse to automate these workflows will continue to burn out staff, lose caregivers, and drain their own time every day.

Manual offices cannot compete with intelligent offices.

The hours lost to administrative work are the first point of collapse.

---

2. Agencies Lose When They Depend on Human Memory

Care plans change.
Tasks change.
Client conditions change.
Family expectations change.
Medication routines change.
Daily patterns shift.

In the old model, everything depends on:

caregiver memory
office memory
notes
calls
and guesswork.

That structure collapses under pressure.

Agencies that refuse to implement intelligent
reminders, pattern recognition, and real-time
updates will continue to experience:

missed tasks
family frustration
compliance issues
and preventable mistakes.

Human memory is not a strategy.
It is a liability.

---

3. Agencies Lose When They Cannot Show Proof

Families are done taking agencies at their word.

They want:

confirmation
visibility
patterns
documentation
and accuracy.

Agencies that cannot show proof will lose:

trust
referrals
clinical partners
care managers
and family confidence.

The agencies that win the next decade are the ones who can prove value, not just promise it.

---

4. Agencies Lose When They Rely on Unpredictable Scheduling

Scheduling is the heartbeat of home care.

But unpredictable scheduling destroys:

caregiver morale
family trust
office stability
and outcomes.

AI-supported scheduling:

predicts conflicts
stabilizes routines
matches patterns
reduces last minute changes
and reduces chaos.

Agencies that refuse this evolution will watch turnover rise until their office collapses under staffing pressure.

Scheduling is no longer an administrative function. It is a competitive advantage.

---

5. Agencies Lose When They Ignore the Caregiver Experience

Caregivers today are not choosing agencies based on:

pay alone
hours alone
geography alone
referrals alone
brand alone.

They are choosing agencies that:

support them
guide them
value them
make their job easier
and reduce their stress.

If an agency does not lighten the caregiver's day, the caregiver will leave.

The agencies that refuse to modernize their caregiver experience will lose every staffing battle.

Caregivers stay where they feel supported.
AI provides that support.
Agencies that ignore it lose the workforce entirely.

---

6. Agencies Lose When They Resist Predictive Safety

Falls
confusion
dehydration
behavior shifts
mobility changes
wandering
sleep disruption.

These patterns do not appear suddenly.

They appear gradually.

Agencies that refuse predictive analytics will continue to:

miss early signs
respond late
face hospital readmissions

deal with family panic
and lose clients.

Early detection is no longer optional.
It is the expectation.

---

7. Agencies Lose When They Cannot Give Families Peace of Mind

Families today want:

notifications
clarity
simple updates
pattern visibility
risk awareness
and proof of stability.

They do not want another phone call saying:

"We are doing our best."
"We did not know."
"No one told us."
"The caregiver forgot to mention it."
"It slipped through the cracks."

Silence is a failure.
Uncertainty is a failure.
Lack of visibility is a failure.

Agencies that refuse to evolve their communication will lose the next generation of digitally fluent families.

---

8. Agencies Lose When They Ignore Economics

The cost structure of the old model is breaking:

office payroll
administrator overload
manual task management
paperwork
training
recruiting
scheduling
compliance.

Agencies that refuse to adopt intelligent systems are choosing an expensive future with shrinking margins.

AI makes the agency lighter.
Ignoring AI makes the agency heavier.

Heavy agencies lose.

---

9. Agencies Lose When PE Consolidation Collapses

Private equity groups buying ten, fifteen, or twenty territories at a time are building an empire on outdated economics.

They are stacking:

administrators
coordinators
regional staffing teams
centralized compliance
high overhead
and manual processes.

When the economics shift, large structures collapse first.

Agencies that model themselves after PE consolidation will get crushed.

The future belongs to:

lean
light
intelligent
adaptive
future ready

operations.

---

10. Agencies Lose When They Confuse Tradition With Strength

Many agencies believe:

"We have always done it this way."

Tradition is not strength.
Tradition is not strategy.
Tradition is not sustainability.

The agencies that cling to tradition will lose market share to agencies that offer:

better communication
better visibility
better consistency
better safety
better support

Families switch when they find something that feels safer.

The future wins because it feels safer.

The Industry Will Not Collapse. The Old Model Will.

Agencies that refuse to adapt will lose:

caregivers
families
reputation
profit
and relevance

Agencies that evolve will gain:

clarity
efficiency
loyalty
peace of mind
stability
and growth.

The choice is not complicated.

Evolve or recede.
Lead or follow.
Transform or be replaced.

Agencies do not lose because of AI.
Agencies lose because they refuse to change.

The future is already moving.
Agencies can move with it or fall behind it.

The market will decide.

Chapter 23: What the Next Decade of Home Care Will Look Like

"The next decade will not be defined by who works the hardest. It will be defined by who builds the smartest."

The future of home care is already forming.
Not in conferences.
Not in franchisor playbooks.
Not in policy memos.
Not in PowerPoint slides.

You can see it in the trends that are accelerating quietly and the cracks that are widening loudly.

The next decade of care will not be a continuation of the last.
It will be a correction and then a transformation.

This chapter is not a prediction.
It is a trajectory.
The patterns are already in motion.

Here is where home care is heading over the next ten years.

---

1. Smaller Agencies Will Outperform Multi-Territory Operators

Scale used to be a strength.
Scale is becoming weight.

Large agencies will buckle under:

coordinator overload
centralized compliance
manual scheduling
office payroll
bureaucracy.

Smaller agencies will win because they will be:

lighter
faster
smarter
leaner
AI-supported.

The future belongs to the agency that can move quickly, not the one that owns the most zip codes.

---

2. The Caregiver Will Become the Center of the Ecosystem

Caregivers have been treated like labor.
They will become treated like talent.

The next decade will bring:

AI-guided support
real-time training
lighter documentation
guided workflows
fewer burdens
safer environments.

Caregivers who feel supported stay.
Caregivers who stay stabilize agencies.
Stabilized agencies dominate markets.

The industry will finally realize that the caregiver is not the problem.
The system around the caregiver is the problem.

---

3. Families Will Drive the Industry, Not Agencies or Franchisors

Families will no longer tolerate:

silence
inconsistent updates
manual processes
paper-driven care
invisible schedules
guesswork.

They will choose agencies that provide:

visibility
predictability
safety

proof
clarity.

Agencies that cannot deliver this will lose families in weeks, not months.

The family is the new payer.
The family is the new quality department.
The family is the new force shaping the market.

---

4. AI Will Become the Standard, Not the Differentiator

In the early years, agencies using AI will stand out. By the end of the decade, agencies without AI will disappear.

AI will become normal the same way:

GPS became normal
online banking became normal
telehealth became normal
digital signatures became normal
automated reminders became normal.

The market will not ask whether an agency uses AI. The market will assume it.

Agencies that resist will become as outdated as paper maps.

---

5. Documentation Will Become Fully Automated

Paper notes and manual entries will not survive.

In the next decade:

caregivers will speak
systems will record
systems will structure
systems will summarize
systems will file
systems will notify.

Documentation will be effortless and accurate.

This reduces liability.
This improves compliance.
This stabilizes operations.
This eliminates chaos.

The agencies that still rely on manual notes will be left behind.

---

6. Safety Will Become Predictive Instead of Reactive

Today, safety depends on luck.

In the next decade, safety will depend on intelligence.

AI will detect:

mobility changes
hydration issues
eating patterns
sleep disruptions
behavioral shifts
environmental risks.

before they turn into emergencies.

Families will expect early detection.
Hospitals will demand it.
Payers will reward it.

Reactive agencies will be phased out.
Predictive agencies will become the industry standard.

---

7. Independent Caregivers Will Rise, But Only with AI Support

The next decade will see the rise of the independent caregiver.

Not the gig model.
Not the directory model.
Not the marketplace model.

A supported model.

Independent caregivers will thrive only when paired with:

risk alerts
training
guided workflows
documentation
visibility
backup support
safety signals.

Agencies will not disappear.
But their role will shift from staffing companies to oversight leaders.

Independent caregivers plus intelligence equals stability.

---

8. The Care Plan Will Become a Living Document

Static care plans will become extinct.

The care plan of the future will:

adapt
shift
update
predict
respond
and learn

with the client.

Families will no longer wait for quarterly reviews.
They will expect daily evolution.

AI will turn the care plan into a real-time guidance system instead of a piece of paper in a binder.

---

9. Operators Will Become Care Architects, Not Crisis Managers

Operators today are trapped in:

staffing
scheduling
paperwork
compliance
panic
exhaustion.

AI eliminates the noise.

Operators of the future will focus on:

interpretation
leadership
oversight
coaching
family engagement
outcomes.

The operators who understand this shift will rise. The ones clinging to crisis management will fade out.

---

10. The Industry Will Split Into Two Categories

By 2035, home care will be divided clearly:

Category 1: Agencies using intelligent systems.
These agencies will be stable, growing, profitable, and predictable.

Category 2: Agencies still running manually.
These agencies will shrink, become overwhelmed, and eventually become noncompetitive.

The split will not be philosophical.
It will be economic.

Intelligence will reduce cost and increase value.
Manual operations will increase cost and reduce value.

The market will decide quickly.

---

11. The Best Agencies Will Be Built by People Who Lived the Pain

The next generation of industry leaders will not come from:

corporate offices
PE firms
franchise development teams
or tech companies

They will come from:

operators
care coordinators
caregivers
nurses
families

The people who have lived the stress will build the tools that remove the stress.

Experience will finally become the foundation for innovation, not an afterthought.

The Next Decade Is Not the Death of Home Care. It Is the Rebuild.

The old model collapses.
The new model emerges.

Care becomes clearer.
Caregivers become supported.
Families become informed.
Operators become leaders.
Agencies become lighter.
Outcomes improve.
Safety strengthens.

The next decade is not destruction.

The next decade is alignment.

For the first time, the system will match the reality of care.

And the operators who understand this early will lead the future.

Chapter 24: The System We Build Now

"The future does not wait for permission. It waits for builders."

We are standing at the edge of the most important shift in the history of home care.

Not a policy shift.
Not a reimbursement shift.
Not a franchise shift.
Not a technology trend.

A structural shift.

The old model is collapsing quietly.
The new model is forming loudly.
And the people who have lived the pressure of this industry are finally ready to build something that fits the world we actually live in.

This chapter is not a conclusion.
It is a beginning.

This is the system we build now.

---

1. We Build a System Where Caregivers Are Supported, Not Stretched

Caregivers have always been expected to carry the weight no human being should carry alone.

They carried:

documentation
unclear instructions
unsafe homes
emotional labor
last-minute changes
family expectations
and system failures.

The new model removes that weight.

We build a system where:

training is real-time
documentation is automated
safety is predictive
support is constant
burnout is prevented
and the caregiver is finally treated like the center of the ecosystem.

Caregivers deserve a model that protects them.

We build that now.

---

2. We Build a System Where Families Get Clarity Instead of Confusion

Families have lived in uncertainty for too long.

They have been forced to guess.
Forced to hope.
Forced to wait.
Forced to worry.

The new model eliminates silence.

We build a system where families get:

visibility
updates
proof
support
early detection
and peace.

Families deserve transparency and truth, not
fragments of information.

We build that now.

---

3. We Build a System Where Operators Finally Lead Instead of React

Operators today are buried under a mountain of
noise.

Calls.
Schedules.
Paperwork.
Crises.
Turnover.

Compliance.
Fatigue.

They are leaders trapped in survival mode.

The new model lifts the weight so operators can finally lead.

We build a system where operators become:

architects
coaches
strategists
stability partners
and outcome leaders

Operators deserve a model that honors the work they pour into this industry.

We build that now.

---

4. We Build a System Where Intelligence Carries the Administrative Weight

No industry can survive long-term when humans carry more weight than systems.

Home care has reached that limit.

The new model shifts the load from people to intelligence.

Scheduling.
Documentation.
Risk alerts.
Family communication.
Care plan updates.
Training guidance.
Pattern recognition.

Intelligence carries the burden so humans can carry the care.

This is not replacing people.
It is protecting them.

We build that now.

---

5. We Build a System That Adapts Instead of Breaks

The old model treated care like a fixed routine.

The new model treats care like a living process.

It adapts.
Learns.
Responds.
Anticipates.
Evolves.
Supports.

Static systems break.
Adaptive systems last.

We build the adaptive system now.

---

6. We Build a System That Honors the Reality of Aging

Aging today is not what it was twenty years ago.

People are:

older
sicker
more isolated
more dependent
and living longer than the system was ever designed to support.

The old model cannot stretch far enough to meet this reality.

The new model can.

We build a system that matches the truth of modern aging.
Not the assumptions of an outdated past.

---

7. We Build a System That Turns the Care Plan Into a Living Guide

Families need guidance.
Caregivers need clarity.
Operators need visibility.

The care plan becomes the central brain of the entire ecosystem.

It updates in real time.
It reflects patterns.
It suggests interventions.
It shifts with conditions.
It learns from the day.

This is where care becomes safer, calmer, and more predictable.

We build that now.

---

8. We Build a System Where Outcomes Improve Because Everyone Is Supported

When caregivers are supported, quality rises.
When families are informed, trust rises.
When operators have clarity, stability rises.
When documentation is accurate, safety rises.
When intelligence sees patterns, outcomes rise.

The industry improves when the people inside it are supported.

Support is the new infrastructure.

We build that now.

---

9. We Build a System That Finally Makes Sense

For the first time, home care will align with:

how families live
how caregivers work
how technology functions
how aging evolves
and how risk unfolds

Care will become:

predictable
visible
structured
coordinated
supported
and humane.

This is the model home care has needed for decades.

We build it now.

The Quiet Collapse Is Not the End. It Is the Beginning.

We are not writing an obituary for home care.
We are writing the blueprint for what replaces it.

The old model collapses because it reached its limit.
The new model rises because it removes the weight.

Care becomes clearer.
Caregivers become stronger.

Families become calmer.
Operators become leaders.
Agencies become lighter.
Outcomes become better.

The future is not something we wait for.

The future is something we build.

Quietly.
Intentionally.
One system at a time.
One day at a time.
One moment of care at a time.

This is the system we build now.

This is the future of home care.

And it is nothing to fear.

EPILOGUE

Why I Wrote This

I wrote this because I care.

For almost two decades, I have lived inside this industry. I have seen the best of it and the worst of it. I have seen caregivers show up for families when no one else would. I have seen operators lose themselves trying to hold broken systems together. I have seen families walk into home care with hope and leave with exhaustion.

And for a long time, I thought my time in this industry was coming to an end.

In 2018, I sold one of my offices and almost walked away completely. I was worn down by the pressure, the staffing struggles, the shrinking margins, and the constant feeling that everyone was surviving instead of building. I thought I was done.

But I realized something.
It was still a great business.
And I brought value.

I knew how to operate at a high level.
I knew how to build systems.
I knew how to protect caregivers and deliver quality for families.
I knew what worked and what broke things.

That is why I wrote my first book, *Built From Scratch: How to Launch and Grow a Successful Non-Medical Home Care Agency*. I wrote it because I saw too many operators entering the industry with passion but no blueprint. I watched good people burn out because they were working inside a model that demanded more than anyone could give.

I never believed home care was failing because people did not care.
I believed it was failing because the structure was outdated.

And for years, I waited for the industry to catch up.
I went to conferences.
I sat in leadership rooms.
I listened to keynote speakers talk about the future.

But I kept hearing the same thing.
Motivation. Marketing. Recruitment.

What I did not hear was innovation.

I remember the last conference I attended.
AI was transforming every industry on the planet, yet it was barely mentioned in a room full of people who claimed to be preparing for the future. That was the moment I decided something had to change.

I stopped waiting for someone else to build what caregivers needed.
I stopped waiting for franchisors to innovate.
I stopped waiting for national leaders to lead.

I told myself, I am going to do something about this.

Because I have always believed the caregiver is the center point.
Not the agency.
Not the franchisor.
Not the software.

The caregiver.
The person who shows up in the home.
The person who carries the emotional, physical, and human weight of care.

And I have said for years that the system should be built around them, not the other way around. But no one wanted to shift the structure because it threatened the comfort of the past.

So I wrote this book to say what needed to be said.
I wrote it to put the truth on the table.
I wrote it to push the conversation forward.
I wrote it so no one can pretend the future is unclear.

This industry is not dying.
It is transforming.
And the people who lead the next decade will be the ones who are brave enough to let go of the old and build what comes next.

I wrote this for the caregivers who deserve support.
I wrote this for the families who deserve clarity.
I wrote this for the operators who are tired of carrying all the weight.

I wrote this for the policymakers who want solutions, not slogans.
I wrote this for anyone who believes care can be better than what we have accepted.

This is not the end of home care.
It is the beginning of a new chapter.
A chapter that puts intelligence behind the people who give care, not in front of them.

The system will change.
The model will evolve.
And the future will belong to the people who choose to build it.

This is where the old story ends.
This is where the new one begins.

ABOUT THE AUTHOR

Brian B. Turner is a writer, strategist, and industry innovator who has spent almost two decades studying the structure, pressures, and future of the non-medical home care system. His work explores how caregiving can evolve through better design, smarter operations, and technology that strengthens both the workforce and the families who depend on it.

He is the author of *Built From Scratch: How to Launch and Grow a Successful Non-Medical Home Care Agency*, a widely used resource among new and established home care leaders. His writing brings clarity to an industry under pressure and offers a forward-thinking view of what sustainable care must look like in the years ahead.

Brian's mission is to support the people inside the care economy by challenging old assumptions, amplifying new ideas, and building frameworks that make caregiving more stable, more transparent, and more human. He writes and speaks about innovation, operational excellence, and the emerging role of AI in shaping the future of home care.